The Success Playbook for Next Gen Family Business Leaders

Book #1 in the Next Gen Family Business Leadership Series

Doug Gray, PhD

Testimonials:

"If you need practical wisdom, based on Doug's Family Business research and decades of consulting, then I recommend you buy and share this book."
Rich Wolkowitz, Founder, Xylogenesis Family Business Advisory

"This book is a great practical guide with valuable tips and references all through. An easy read with a lifetime of wisdom on these pages. Easy for me to recommend!" *John Broons, Family Business Advisor, Australia*

"Doug's coaching and support during our multi-year leadership transition has proved to be invaluable. Family business transitions can be complex, Doug has positioned our Next Gen leaders to better address challenges and take advantage of new opportunities in the future. Most importantly, Doug is all about ACTION. While our transition is complete, I'll be working with Doug for years to come to continue to learn and grow as a leader in our business."
Rawleigh Taylor, non-family Chief Revenue Officer, CSC Leasing

"I like that this workbook starts with and emphasizes the "individual" – the most important unit in family business systems. This a great resource for both current and Next Gen leaders."
Richa Singh, Consultant, The Family Business Consulting Group

"A robust compendium of pragmatic wisdom and best practices that will benefit leaders and members of family businesses of all shapes and sizes."
Jonathon Thompson, non-family CEO, Nielsen-Massey Vanillas

"I appreciate how the Individual is emphasized in this 5 system model. This book is a must read for Next Gen individuals who are working in a family enterprise or considering working in their family enterprise. Some individuals will be energized to develop the skills required to navigate the complex nature of Family Enterprises and others may recognize their skills, abilities and interests are better suited elsewhere. Regardless of which path you take, you will gain appreciation for the leadership, management, and interpersonal skills required to build your thriving Family Enterprise."

Jake Knight, G2 family leader, CEO Enclave

"From one the most astute family business gurus, Doug Gray, come ten practical "plays" for navigating the most important arenas of business. This short but powerful work is organized around actionable principles for building business value while prizing the family relationships. Doug also provides curated suggestions for deeper dives and further reading." *Charles Glick, Chairman & CEO, Corporate Governance Partners*

Copyright © 2024 by Doug Gray, PhD, PCC All rights reserved.

Thank you for purchasing an authorized copy of this book and for complying with international copyright law. No part of this book may be reproduced or used in any manner without the prior written consent of the copyright owner, except for the use of brief quotations in a book review.

The information contained in this book is not intended as a substitute for expert services or consultation with any financial, legal, or business consultants. All readers have unique circumstances that require specific expertise and customized solutions. All names included in this text are changed to protect the confidential identities of my clients.

Published by Gray Publications, a product of Action Learning Associates, LLC. Book #1 in the Next Gen Family Business Leadership Series.

For consulting, bulk ordering information, or to request permissions, contact www.Action-Learning.com at 3482 Stagecoach Drive, Franklin, TN, USA.

For additional digital content go to
https://www.nextgenpeergroups.com/gifts

For assessments go to https://assessnextgen.com/

eBook ISBN-13: 978-0-9758841-3-3 for $6.97 USD
Paperback ISBN-13: 978-0-9758841-8-8 for $19.97 USD

Copy editing by Kristen Weber at KW Anderson
Cover design and interior formatting by eBookLaunch
Cartoons are copyrighted and used with permission from Glasbergen

Contents

Introduction 1
First Steps 4
The Next Gen Model 5
The Science 9
Chapter 1: The Individual System 12
Chapter 2: The Family System 36
Chapter 3: The Business System 58
Chapter 4: The Learning System 74
Chapter 5: The Ownership System 93
Next Steps 112
Appendix 1. Your Personalized Learning Plan (PLP) 114
Appendix 2. Assumptions for the Five Systems 115
Appendix 3: The Leadership 360 Assessment Process 117
Appendix 4: Family Business Consulting Group (FBCG) Resources for YOU sorted by the five systems 120
Appendix 5: My Published articles 124
Appendix 6: Book List 130
List of Key Definitions 135
About the Author 141
Consulting Services 142

Introduction

You may know that family businesses drive most of the Gross Domestic Product (GDP) and job creation in every country.

You probably know examples of family businesses, from agriculture to finance, from banking to hotels, from manufacturing to retail. ***Family businesses are the social fabric of every community, throughout history, in every corner of the world.***

Sadly, too many family business leaders don't know how to transfer their financial and capital assets. The largest wealth transfer in human history is happening right now. My experience is that too many of those leaders are confused.

Older family business leaders tell me, "I can't sleep. I don't know who is capable of taking over my business. And frankly, I don't know what else I'd do."

Younger family business leaders tell me, "I'm tired of waiting. I've done everything I've been asked to do. I'm stuck in the middle. Our people sometimes think I'm in charge, but I still need to get approvals from my father or the owners."

Both of those groups need this short Success Playbook!

Older family business leaders need to give up control and develop their multi-generational purpose or legacy. You are an important audience for this book.

Younger family business leaders need to practice all of these 10 behaviors, so that YOU gain clarity about your career, succession, and next steps. You are the primary audience for this book.

The word "YOU" is capitalized throughout this playbook because I invite YOU to play with these ideas. Regardless of your age and role! Also, the word "practice" is used about 147 times in this short playbook... because I want you to play with these practices.

The **Goal** of this Success Playbook is to **TRANSFORM ALL FAMILY BUSINESS LEADERS,** young and old.

Next Gen leaders like you have always struggled to assess your strengths and weaknesses, to share your capacity, or to prove your ability to take on responsibilities.

Did you know that today's generation of Next Gen leaders is better educated than any in recorded human history? You will probably live longer. You will have more career choices. You will continue to embrace complexity. You are more digitally trusting. And you are as hopeful about your inheritance as any generation in time.

Did you know that **today we are experiencing the largest transfer of wealth in human history- at least $74 trillion USD**? Many of my clients struggle to identify how their Next Gen (or Rising Gen) leaders can assume responsibility for that wealth. And too many Next Gen leaders wonder how they can prove their capabilities.

Most of the economies in every corner of the world are determined by Family Business leaders on Main Streets and home offices— not on Wall Street. This book is designed for the "Mom and Pop" businesses on Main Street as well as those with global capital and financial investments.

Family businesses describe over 65% of the gross domestic product (GDP) in the United States, and higher percentages in Europe and Asia. Family businesses drive **over 70% of new jobs.** But those facts do not necessarily suggest that anyone is sleeping better at night!

YOU need career clarity. You need this Success Playbook.

A playbook, by definition, is a set of tested actions for individuals and teams to achieve a shared goal. In sports like football, the offensive team needs both a running game and a passing game to put points on the scoreboard. The defensive team needs to protect yardage with as few plays as possible. In family business consulting, leaders need a playbook that decreases complexity and conflict, and increases communication and succession. This playbook is based on my globally validated research and decades of consulting with hundreds of family and non-family leaders. Let's go!

First Steps

To get started, here are YOUR first steps:

1. Take the self-rater or 360 Leadership Assessment survey at www.AssessNextGen.com to identify your strengths, weaknesses, blind spots/gaps, and hidden strengths. A link to that self-rater is at https://www.nextgenpeergroups.com/gifts

2. List your highest scores, your top 3-4 strengths here so that you stay focused on developing them:

_____

_____

_____

_____

3. List your lowest scores, your bottom 3-4 weaknesses here so that you can focus on developing them:

_____

_____

_____

_____

4. Use the Personalized Learning Plan (PLP) in the Appendix to
   - Practice with your consultant or accountability coach
   - Practice with your Next Gen Peer Group network (see details at www.NextGenPeerGroups.com)
   - Practice with your colleagues
   - Practice with your family/friends/champions
   - Develop these behaviors ASAP
   - Celebrate at each milestone!

THE NEXT GEN MODEL

Theoretical models are pictures designed to simplify complexity.

For example, as a behavioral psychologist, I **focus on what people say or do**. And I've been consulting since 1997 with hundreds of business leaders.

I've learned that **Family Enterprises** are more complex than any other type of business, so my model describes the complex relationships of five systems—the individual, family, business, learning and ownership systems. See Figure 1.

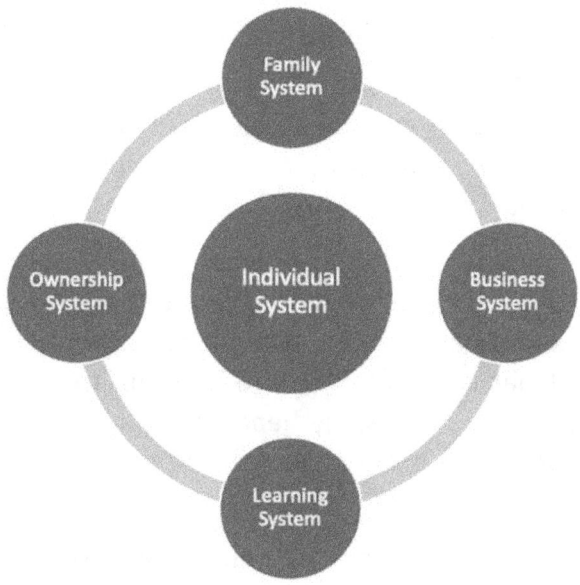

Figure 1. The Assess Next Gen™ model for Family Business leaders

This model provides the skeletal system for this Success Playbook. And each reader, YOU, provide the life blood for your family business.

There are two central questions for every leader:

1. **How do I fit in?**
2. **What is my capability?**

Hmmm.

YOU may not be able to answer those questions, yet. That's OK.

Your family is uniquely complex. Just like everyone else's family! Just like every Family Business or Enterprise, you are unique and complex.

The first three roles are usually easy to describe- as a **family** member, and/or **business** member and/or **owner**. Those roles describe the "Three Hats" you may be wearing. The hats may change, and those three roles describe most family and non-family leaders.

Family members are usually defined by bloodlines or those who married in, and may or may not include domestic partners or widows.

Business members are those who actively work in the business to provide a product or service to a customer. Family members often have an employment guideline process that describes what is required before applying to work in the family business. Non-family leaders typically outnumber family leaders, and bring expertise and scale as businesses evolve.

Owners determine the strategy and asset distributions for any perceived risks or rewards. They carry the responsibility for continuity, legacy, mergers, etc. Most wealth is quietly transferred from owners to the next generation using a succession process based on vision, mission, goals and measures. That process is the most effective form of wealth transfer in every corner of the world. The details are often confidential, which is why business degree programs do not focus on family businesses.

When I use this model with clients, someone often states "I'm an owner!"

Then someone has to state, "No, honey, sorry."

You may think like an owner, but not be an owner according to your shareholder agreement.

You may be an in-law and think you're family, until there is a divorce or liquidity event according to bloodline. You may think you're in the business, until there is a failure or sale. Those three systems are necessary to describe most family businesses, but they are incomplete.

The **Learning System** describes how you adapt to new information, like this Success Playbook. Adult learners are driven by curiosity. Adult learners read short books and practice agility. 100% of my clients work in learning organizations. You know that your competitive advantage includes investing in your people. You are reading this so that you can do whatever it takes to succeed.

The BIG struggle for all Next Gen leaders— both family and non-family — is to determine how YOU fit into your unique family. The **Individual System** is the center of this model for many reasons. It's the biggest circle. It's the most critical system for succession and continuity. That struggle is also the backbone of social psychology, industrial-organizational (I/O) psychology, and human maturity.

Just as children fit into a system, Next Gen leaders like you fit into a system.

HOW do YOU fit into YOUR family system?

That's the central question of this book!

There are five answers to that question, described in each of these five chapters and based on my global research.

For each of these five systems, YOU will see the assumptions that I used when developing the behaviors in the Assess Next Gen™ leadership 360 consulting process.

Then you will see **the top two behaviors,** based on my research with hundreds of leaders, and many practical suggestions for you. There's over 100 years of research in the social sciences, but little research in family business systems. Here's a little bit of science to get you started.

The Science

What is the Assess Next Gen™ Consulting Process?

In response to client requests and a perceived market opportunity, Kent Rhodes, Ed.D. and I developed and validated a digital 360 consulting process for Next Gen Family Business leaders in 2022.

We started with the theoretical model that reflects the complexity of family enterprises and the need for individual fit (Figure 1). Those five systems are familiar: the business, family, ownership, individual and learning system. Systems theory is not new. However, psychometric validation of those five systems required that we identified 250 behavior items, then statistically reduced that number to 10 items in each system, using a global sample population. The result is a new validated 50-item behavior-based digital 360 assessment process for next generation family business leaders.

360 assessments are the most valid performance feedback process known to organizational development psychologists.

This assessment process is now defined by best practices for rigor, confidentiality and relevance. Raters may have multiple roles. For example, Uncle Bob may be an owner and a manager and a family member. This assessment process includes seven rater groups, and a hierarchy that reflects the complexity in many family enterprises. Uncle Bob should provide feedback as an owner (first). Those seven rater groups include owners, board members, managers, peers, direct reports, family/friends, and self-raters. The overall scores (high and low behaviors) and the gaps between other ratings and self-ratings, provide critical behaviors for the next gen leader, and the owners, to make strategic decisions. The consulting process is both quantitative (using at least 13 raters) and qualitative (using verbatim comments and behavioral interviews).

We have validated two versions: one for non-family leaders and one for family leaders. And we have a self-rater version for any leader in a family business. For additional digital content go to https://www.nextgenpeergroups.com/gifts

This leadership assessment process provides invaluable direction for a consultant, deep behavioral insight for the owners and board, models performance feedback and organizational change, and clarifies required behaviors for any decision-makers included in this process.

Figure 2 describes the seven steps in our Assess Next Gen™ Consulting process.

Figure 2. The Assess Next Gen™ Consulting Process

My experience with hundreds of leaders is that any advisors serving family enterprises can benefit from this 360 leadership assessment process. We now have process guidelines for consistent delivery of behavioral feedback for licensees.

There is no more need for sleepless nights, either for owners or for Next Gen leaders!

I often state, "We all need a little structure." This process provides both direction and intensity for any Next Gen leader.

There are more details in the appendix for those who want more science and my published articles.

How should YOU to use this Playbook?

Use this Success Playbook like a workbook or a cookbook.

Sample one chapter at a time. Take notes. Skip pages. Come back to the next chapter when useful. Adults learn best when you sample ideas, practice them in practical ways, get emotionally engaged, and share ideas with others.

Learning is haphazard and emotional. We learn when we laugh. That's why each of these five systems starts with a cartoon.

Yes! YOU can play with this playbook!

Let's get started...

Chapter 1: The Individual System

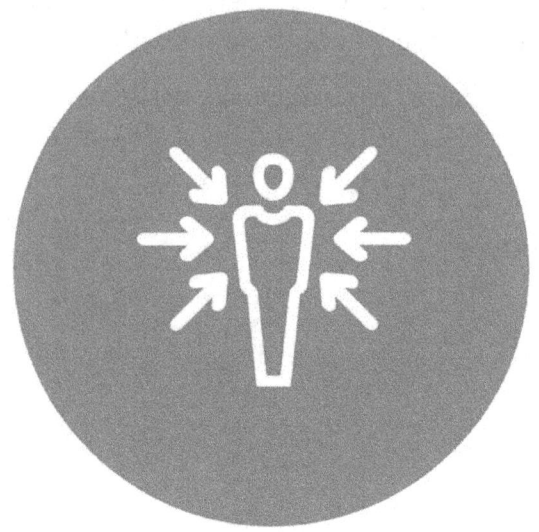

The top two key behaviors:

1. Express my thoughts and feelings on important topics.
2. Express a positive attitude.

My assumptions for the Individual System:

1. You have agency/ choice
2. You have the capacity to flourish
3. Your individual awareness drives your behaviors and career(s)
4. Practicing leadership requires both knowing/awareness and showing/actions

You may not like or agree with these assumptions. My experience is that assumptions lead to behaviors! So, for this playbook, it makes sense to look at the top two behaviors for the Individual System.

Then you can play with these two behaviors!

Here are many great tactics and "plays" for you to consider.

"There is no *I* in *TEAM*. But there is an *M* and an *E* and that spells *ME!*"

1. Express my thoughts and feelings on important topics.

This is the MOST important behavior for **individual family business** leaders, based on my research to date.

We ALL need to bite our tongues, especially when emotions or judgments can increase conflict.

The question is: **How do YOU know when to speak up, and when to shut up?**

Here's a great guideline. If **any** of these ground rules are broken, then YOU need to speak up.

I've used these ground rules for decades:

1. Be here now
2. Assume positive intent in others
3. Listen to understand
4. Provide honest feedback
5. Celebrate what works
6. Keep our humor 😊

Here are some "yellow flag" or "red flag" comments from frustrated Next Gen family business leaders. Listen for these kinds of statements!

"I often feel hesitant to speak up because I fear my thoughts and feelings will be dismissed."

"It's frustrating when others dominate the conversation, leaving no space for my input."

"I wish I had the confidence to express my ideas and opinions without fearing judgment."

These **trigger statements** can help you today. If you hear any of these type of statements, then use them as triggers to state your thoughts and emotions.

Or use these type of statements to ask for more information. **One of my favorite coaching questions is, "Tell me more…"**

The focus of this individual behavior is HOW.

HOW do you express your thoughts and feelings on important topics?

Here are four tips that work well. Play with them…

1. Build Self-Awareness

We all need to exhale. We all need to look in the mirror. All good **leadership development models start with self-awareness**, so it makes sense that this success playbook starts with self-awareness.

You can start by developing a deeper understanding of your own thoughts and feelings. You can take time for self-reflection and journaling. You can explore your opinions and emotions on new topics. Your level of self-awareness will give you the confidence to express yourself authentically.

Self-awareness requires that YOU are open to feedback from others or from assessments that are both reliable and valid. One of the best free assessments is at https://www.viacharacter.org/ (funded by the Meyerson Family Foundation). If you take that assessment, then you will have the vocabulary words to describe your strengths. Then you can study them. And practice your strengths.

Self-awareness changes as we age, and requires that we get feedback from others. Your Uncle Greg or Founder may be rigid, unaware of his blind spots, and unwilling to listen or grow... But **YOU can never change other people.** That would be a waste of time and energy. When you do you, then you will grow.

One more point: **Self-deception** is the inaccurate narrative we create based on low self-awareness or inaccurate feedback from others. Be careful- *we all need to avoid self-deception*, and increase accurate self-awareness. All the time.

2. Practice Active Listening

Yes, I know that I have two ears and know that I should listen better. Of course! But how do I do that when my brother is speaking nonsense?

Active listening is a skill that we can all develop over time. As marriage counselors know, active listening is a skill that predicts whether couples will break up, or will work things out.

YOU can pause before expressing your own thoughts. The research is clear. Practice the pause (More details are below). I use digital timers, or an hourglass from a board game, to make sure that people don't speak too much.

Many of my clients like the **RASA model: Receive. Appreciate. Summarize. Ask.**

This RASA model is easy to practice using all four steps. The **Receive Step** means that YOU have to lean forward, look others in the eye, and open your emotions and judgements to decipher WHAT and HOW the other person is speaking. The **Appreciate Step** requires that you encourage others with vocal pauses like "yes" or "tell me more." The **Summarize Step** often starts with the word "so" followed by your understanding of what the other person was sharing— their words, tone, emotions. The **Ask Step** requires that you confirm that your summary was in fact accurate. So often we don't practice active listening. But you can develop active listening.

That's why YOU are reading this Success Playbook!

There are no certification programs for active listening… it is a skill that requires practice. Reflection is good. Mirrors are pretty good reinforcement tools.

But **the best behavioral feedback tool in human history is a digital screen** such as Zoom, MicroSoft Teams, or Facetime. I use those digital screens every day to notice HOW others communicate and to self-manage HOW I should interact.

I use a Postix note to remind me to focus on others, and their agenda. The Postix note say **"WAISN?"** which stands for **"Why Am I Speaking Now?"** That Postix helps me be a better active listener.

Try it. As a little experiment...

You can notice how others respond when you practice active listening skills such as looking attentive, asking for clarification, summarizing, disagreeing, and validating others. My experience is that your loved ones and colleagues will notice a difference within weeks.

3. Choose the Right Time and Place

When your cousin or sister-in-law says something stupid on social media, what do you do?

We all get triggered in different ways. You may notice those **triggers somewhere in your body**. One cousin may be a "pain in the neck" and another cousin may be "nauseating." Conflicts happen when you respond poorly to those triggers.

The phrase I often share with clients is ***"Trigger. Pause. Respond."*** When you forget to pause, then you perpetuate conflicts. "Ready, Aim, Fire" becomes something bad, like "Ready, Fire, Aim" or "Crawl, Run, Walk."

YOU can practice the pause.

Soldiers and high-crisis workers practice the ***Freeze Frame*** technique. Start by taking 7 seconds to freeze your body and mind. Then imagine an energizing image or picture, like your loved ones at a birthday party or some personal victory. Then survey the scene for objective dangers, like gunfire or burning timbers! Then respond carefully. With practice, you can reduce that skill from 7 seconds to a milli-second.

Then you can leap out of a helicopter or into a family meeting.

Timing is crucial when expressing your thoughts and feelings. I often say that on good days I'm able to do three things: **"Create space, Manage pace, and Practice grace."**

You can create the **space**, in private settings where you can practice open and honest discussions. You can avoid confrontational environments or situations where emotions may be running high.

The ancient adage is **"Praise in Public. Criticize in Private."** Perhaps that belongs on another Postix reminder!

You create better spaces when you use direct meetings- NOT chat, email, or voicemail to provide critical feedback to others.

Too often, so-called "constructive feedback" is abused to deconstruct or disempower people. That's why YOU need to create the **private space** for honest discussions.

One advantage of hybrid work environments is that you may be able to **schedule the time and place** for your direct meeting. You can schedule the **pace** when you, and the other person, have self-managed your emotions or judgments.

Time does NOT heal all wounds. That's a silly myth. In fact, we are animals who survive conflict, and fears drive most of our behaviors. Many of my clients describe abusive behaviors from their family of origin, or something cruel stated decades ago. That's why you need to **schedule the pace** of your discussions with others, especially family members.

Grace can only happen after people know that they are safe (physically, professionally, emotionally, psychologically) and can expect dignity, defined as respectful validation. My experience is that churches and schools do a better job of practicing grace than some families. That's why you need to practice sharing your thoughts and emotions with grace.

4. Use "I" Statements

Sometimes we bite our tongues and don't share our thoughts or emotions because we don't know HOW to do so. We need a script. The result is conflict. Here are three communication scripts that have helped hundreds of my clients, and they can help YOU immediately.

When **sharing your opinions, use "I" statements to express your thoughts and feelings without sounding confrontational.** For example, say, "I feel concerned about this issue because…" or "I believe we should consider…" This script promotes open dialogue and reduces defensiveness. It gives people "a rock to hide behind" because they know that it's (only) your opinion.

Another **behavioral script** is to state, "I feel (state emotion) when you (state an undesirable behavior), and I wish you could (state a desirable behavior)." This script has been used for countless generations by parents and by therapists. When your brother triggers you, say "I feel silenced when you cut me off while I'm speaking. I wish you would wait at least 2 seconds after I speak, or ask clarifying questions, instead of cutting me off." Try this script. It works well with family members.

The third script is called the **Complete Communication Wheel**. This script has saved countless careers and relationships— that's a fact, not an exaggeration. I've used it for decades. And I often provide handouts or laminated training cards that people can keep in their wallets or purses or next to their computers for easy reference.

The complete communication wheel works well with potentially difficult conversations. And it can be applied to compliments as easily as criticisms.

Start by asking, "**May I have two minutes of your time?**" If the other person is not available, then whatever you attempt will be ineffective communication. Schedule the discussion.

The script has five parts: data, emotion, judgment, want, will, and a closing question. Each part has a ratio. The first part is **data**. State the 3-5 facts that are shared understandings, can be validated, and build a series of easy "yes" head nods as you agree with one another. The second part is **emotion**. State only one emotion or feeling that is deeply tied to your big want. The third part is **judgment**. State only one judgment or opinion that is deeply tied to your big want. The fourth part is your BIG **want**, or desired new outcome. The fifth part is 2-3 behaviors that you are **willing** to do to support that new outcome.

Then you ask the closing question, "**What would you like to do next?**" And you quietly wait for their response, because you are complete.

YOU can try any of these three scripts. They work great...

Here are two more comments about the need to share our thoughts and feelings with family and business leaders.

Parent and managers want to foster respectful independence, and that struggle is ancient. Pick any religion or history, from the Olympians and Titans to the family down the street (not yours of course!). As your family struggles, you need to practice being respectful, and voicing your thoughts and emotions. Innovation happens when we try new ideas. And every next generation has new ideas. The rate of innovative technologies demands that you trust your voice and speak up. **Family members** need to speak up. That's why YOU need to play with these tactics.

Business leaders also have to speak up. Most have never been taught HOW to foster respectful communication. The ancient models of top-down management are crumbling as younger workers expect to share their thoughts and feelings at work. Support for mental health is now an expectation at many work environments. By definition, **managers need to maximize the productivity of others.** The core skill of effective managers is coaching. All of us can be better coaches. But few business leaders have been taught HOW to encourage others to speak up. That's why YOU need to practice these tactics.

When you choose to increase self-awareness, practice active listening, choose the right time and place, or use any of the three scripts, then you will be able to express your thoughts and feelings on important topics more effectively.

You may need to adopt this famous phrase by the cultural anthropologist, Margaret Mead, *"**Never doubt that a small group of thoughtful committed individuals can change the world. In fact, it's the only thing that ever has.**"*

When you and your people express their unique voices and contribute to meaningful discussions, then we can ALL drive positive change. Speak up!

Related Books

Brown, B. (2015). *Daring Greatly: How the Courage to Be Vulnerable Transforms the Way We Live, Love, Parent, and Lead.* Penguin Books.

Dugan, A.M., Krone, S.P., Lecouvrie, K., Pendergast, J.M., Kenyon-Rouvinez, D.H., & Schuman, A.M. (2008). *A Woman's Place; The Crucial Roles of Women in Family Business.* Part of the Family Business Consulting Series.

Grant, A. (2023). *Hidden Potential; The Power of Achieving Greater Things.* Viking Press.

Kenyon-Rouvinez, D. & Ward, J. (2005). *Family Business Key Issues.* Palgrave. Part of the Family Business Consulting Series.

Nacht, J. & Greenleaf, G. (2018). *Family Champions and Champion Families: Developing Family Leaders to Sustain the Family Enterprise.* Palgrave.

Walsh, F. (2016). *Strengthening Family Resilience; 3rd Ed.* The Guilford Press.

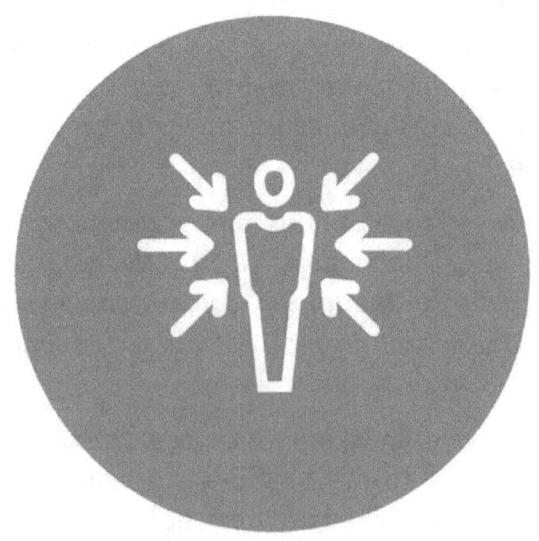

2. Express a positive attitude.

This is one of the MOST important behaviors for **family business** leaders, based on my research to date.

Is that glass half empty or half full? Is that person more optimistic or more pessimistic?

Can you **choose to be more optimistic,** even when you are struggling?

The answer is "YES! Please do so."

The **benefits of choosing a positive attitude** are immense. You will live longer, have deeper relationships, better health, more sales and wealth, and report a higher level of happiness/ subjective well-being.

Don't be like Eeyore in *Winnie The Pooh*. And don't be like Tigger, endlessly bouncing off others. Instead, practice a positive attitude when in public. That's one of the core skills of effective leaders.

Leaders, by definition, influence the behavior of followers toward a positive vision. The core skill of effective leaders is public optimism.

Think of any successful business or social leader.

Gandhi stated, "**Be the change you wish to see in the world.**" As I often add, **"You have no other choice."**

Expressing a positive attitude is a choice.

Do NOT be like the people described below... Instead, practice biting your tongue in public!

"Sometimes it feels like the weight of the world is on my shoulders, and it's challenging to stay positive in the face of adversity."

"I often find myself surrounded by negativity and it takes a toll on my attitude and motivation."

"It's lonely at the top, and maintaining a positive attitude becomes even more difficult when you feel isolated."

You can indeed **"become the change you wish to see in the world."**

Here are some actionable tips and strategies that you can develop with your colleagues and with your consultant. Today! Play with them!

1. **Practice Gratitude**

    Every culture and religion throughout history has habits of gratitude. Examples include prayers, blessing before meals, celebrations like Thanksgiving when the days shorten and our relationships lengthen. We choose to gather with friends, family, colleagues. Then we reflect a bit. And sometimes we over eat…

    The shared habit of **gratitude is to express appreciation for the good things in life.** Gratitude is a skill that requires practice.

    In family business, one current trend for practicing gratitude is called "mindfulness" which can be described as focusing on what fills your mind (positive or negative thoughts) and doing whatever ritual helps you be more intentional in the moment. Related practices include living in the present, savoring, appreciative inquiry, or transcendence.

    You can develop gratitude using the **Three Good Things** activity. It works well, and meets the gold standards of reliability and validity in social psychology with randomly controlled groups.

    Imagine if you selected 100 people and randomly assigned 50 to practice the **Three Good Things** activity every evening before they go to sleep. The task is to **reflect on and write down three good things** that occurred that day. The other 50 people were not invited to write down Three Good Things.

Guess what? Those who practiced the Three Good Things activity consistently report higher levels of happiness, subjective well-being, productivity, relationships, and health than the other group. You can practice the Three Good Things activity today. Give it a try. Share this activity with your children and loved ones.

Look at your **daily rituals**. When you start a family meeting, you may express thanks to your shared faith.

When you start a business meeting you may state recent successes or celebrate what went right. Many of my clients start meetings with a **"Success Minute"** to celebrate what is going well. The rule is to keep it short and only celebrate the work of someone else, NOT boast about your team's success.

When YOU start your day you can express gratitude for the opportunities, relationships, and successes in your life. There is no evidence to suggest those silly digital claims that you need to get up an hour earlier for a particular cleansing ritual. Sleep deprivation only leads to accidents and bad decisions.

For many years I was an expedition adventure racer, and I became expert at managing sleep deprivation.

Imagine being on a team of four athletes, traveling over 500 miles for up to 10 days through a wilderness. Nonstop... Imagine mountain biking, hiking, paddling, climbing cliffs and navigating using only a map and a compass. Imagine the potential conflicts about eating, sleeping, navigation, team dynamics! Imagine only sleeping for 90 minutes on night two, sometime between 3:00 - 5:00 am, so that you could trick your body into thinking that you had enough **deep sleep, in a Rapid Eye Movement (REM) cycle**, that you could keep racing.

Imagine being the team captain, and finishing three expedition races, called Primal Quest, and being on CBS Sports. That's my experience.

When my teams raced through spectacular wilderness landscapes in Washington, Utah and Montana, sometimes I stopped to savor the grandeur. Try it now. Raise your arms in victory. Exhale. Look toward the sun. State something like, "Thank you, God, for all the blessings in my life." That's how you can practice gratitude. It's simple.

There are several digital apps that reinforce gratitude throughout the day, using triggers at different times to remind you to exhale, or to savor the moment. Check out SuperBetter, Daylio, Ultiself and others.

Many of my clients keep a gratitude journal or simply take a moment each day to reflect on the things they are grateful for. You can schedule "**Gratitude Reminder Breaks**" using your smartphone.

This is a simple practice that can shift your mindset in a millisecond and help you maintain a positive attitude. Try it!

2. Surround Yourself with Positivity

How do you respond when someone says, "We can't do that…"?

Negative people reinforce **negativity spirals**, and perpetuate fixed mindsets. Negative people use killer statements like "we tried that" or "in the real world" to shut down innovation. They often cut down others using slander and gossip. And negativity spirals are contagious, because they reinforce what won't work, by using objections and repeating limited beliefs. Negative people kill innovation.

In contrast, **positivity spirals encourage people to "broaden their options and build solutions."**

Positivity is a choice. Just as people can learn to be helpless, they can learn to be optimistic, which is defined as a general, positive view of life. The best research is called **Positive Psychology,** now used in behavioral economics by business leaders everywhere. The most famous researcher, Marty Seligman, started by studying learned helplessness, and now describes himself as a reluctant optimist. There are great free digital resources at Authentic Happiness (Pennsylvania) and Greater Good (Berkely). But this is NOT intended to be an academic book… Let's return to the Success Playbook tactics.

YOU can practice positivity. Positivity spirals are contagious. **Pick 3-5 values that you want to reinforce.** They may NOT be the values of your founders, but they may be similar. Many of my family business clients pick values like loyalty and outstanding service, and those values are critical. Those values got your family business from G1 to G2 or more.

What if you **add values like collaboration, learning agility and humility to your list?** Those are three competencies that will never be replaced by Artificial Intelligence (AI), and they will determine how successful YOUR team can be. Many of my clients use positive behaviors to measure desired performance.

Another list of values is the HERO model, which measures **Hope, Efficacy, Resilience and Optimism.** Notice how you score on these four short questions:

Hope. I believe that I have "the will and the way" to achieve my goals. (1-10)

Efficacy. I feel confident that I know what I need to do to achieve my goals. (1-10)

Resilience. I can get through difficult times or challenges. (1-10)

Optimism. I am optimistic about what will happen to me in the future. (1-10)

Now notice your scores. They provide a baseline for you to determine if you need to practice new behaviors.

Those HERO scores also describe teams. Select the 5-6 people you work with who define your success. Those people have important relationships or skills that are critically important for your success. Notice the scores for those 5-6 people, and for the team.

The research findings are clear. **Successful teams score higher on the HERO model, and teams with low scores can develop higher HERO scores.** (See the books listed below by Luthans for details on Psychological Capital.)

You can surround yourself with positive people who uplift and inspire you. You can avoid negative influences and toxic environments that bring you down. Pessimistic people should be educated or removed from your family business.

You can seek out mentors, colleagues, or friends who demonstrate resilience. Their energy will rub off on you and help you maintain a positive attitude.

Every successful team- in business, life, or sports- describes their shared belief that they can excel. All innovators are optimistic.

3. Reframe Challenges as Opportunities

This behavior is more than a name change or a different label. All human behavior is rooted in our thoughts and emotions.

If you believe that you will fail, then YOU will fail. Repeatedly.

If you believe that you can learn from any challenge, then YOU will succeed. Repeatedly.

You may have heard the cliché, "Every setback is an opportunity for a comeback." The truth behind that cliché is that **your mindset determines your problem sets.**

My experience is that all successful business leaders have an opportunistic belief system. They choose to believe that they can succeed where others have failed. That's what founders do!

Risk tolerance is defined as your willingness to do x instead of losing y. We determine risk costs and reward benefits in a millisecond, because we are expert at surviving threats. I imagine that my great grandparents, like yours, were great at surviving threats. They must have been, because you and I are here today!

Risk avoidance is the opposite, when leaders choose to avoid an innovation because "that's the way we've always done it around here." Risk avoidance is typically an excuse that depends on fear of a loss. For instance, "we can't afford to invest in cybersecurity" or "we don't need to provide day care for our employees." The fact is that **cybersecurity threatens the existence** of most of my clients, and **day care compensation** has the highest ROI for employee engagement. YOU may need to re-think the risks you are currently avoiding!

Loss aversion is a cognitive bias that influences most leaders to avoid any loss- real or imagined- at any cost. We protect what we think are assets against anything that may lead to a future loss. So, how do you avoid loss aversion and take smarter risks?

The research is clear: **most family business leaders need to take more risks.** When Older Generation leaders are surveyed, they regret being risk averse. Next Gen leaders typically favor risk tolerance and innovation.

You may want to add a new product or service, market to a different target, or invest in new digital technologies. Typically, Next Gen leaders are impatient, because you may see returns that others do not see, or because you want to "leave your mark" on the business.

Typically, **Older Generation leaders are loss averse.** They say "No, not know" because they do not want to lose their gains or assets. They have fought hard for their success. Legacy typically becomes even more important as they age.

Instead of seeing challenges as roadblocks, you need to reframe them as opportunities for growth and learning.

History is on your side, because **most innovation comes from small businesses,** not from publicly traded organizations described in Forbes or The Wall Street Journal. **Innovation is best described as "a new idea applied."** That's a simple definition that you can adopt today!

YOU can embrace a growth mindset that views setbacks as stepping stones to success.

You can look for the "silver lining in every situation" and focus on finding solutions rather than dwelling on problems. To be clear, this is a growth attitude- and does NOT ignore the obvious challenges in business or life.

The best examples come from teams, like the military, that conduct lengthy **After-Action Reviews** (AARs) after any activity.

Imagine that a fighter pilot just completed a 2-hour reconnaissance flight. Hundreds of people have contributed to that flight, and the pilot is the "point of the spear." When they meet in an AAR, they need to learn what worked and what needs to be improved. The first to speak are the youngest or most junior officers, and the last to speak is the most senior officer. They are reframing challenges as opportunities.

Now imagine if your leadership team did an AAR or a **Review Meeting** for the last quarter of sales, marketing, operations, or that key project.

YOU can lead regular Review Meetings for your family business immediately. Every successful leader throughout history has learned from their mistakes and embraced new opportunities with open eyes. Try it.

4. Practice Self-Care

Athletes are intentional about self-care because their performance demands consistency.

Business athletes, like you and your colleagues, demand a similar level of high consistency.

Those levels of self-care are often described using interlocking circles, like clouds in the sky or doodles on a mind map. Start with paper and start doodling. **Your self-care labels may include "physically, mentally, emotionally, spiritually, fiscally, interpersonally, professionally"...** or whatever you value. Start doodling!

If you were to **draw a mind map doodle of what YOU do for self-care**, then you can assess your score, using 1-10 numbers, or note your strengths and gaps. Many of my clients do this activity quarterly, to sketch where they are and where they need to go.

You may have had a grandmother or mentor who reminded you to "brush your teeth, make your bed, and eat your vegetables." In the same way, you need to select activities that bring you joy and relaxation, such as exercising, meditating, reading, or pursuing hobbies.

If you enjoy playing golf, then you may hit two large buckets of balls without any fatigue. That state of "**Flow Optimization**" is defined as the balance between challenge and skill. You may not notice that two hours passed while you hit those golf balls. Or when you wrote that proposal. Or developed that project...

The **psychology of flow states** is significant because YOU can select self-care activities that are good for you, like exercise, or bad for you, like excessive video gaming.

One of my 45-year-old clients stated, "I play video games every night because I get to see my score and blow up stuff." He is representative of countless people who spend an average of 6 hours daily on gaming activities. The neurotransmitter and hormone, called **dopamine, reinforces all flow state behaviors.**

That's why I enjoy trail runs or bike rides with friends!

Balance matters. For every exhalation, you need to inhale.

Sleep deprivation leads to accidents and bad judgments. Fast food diets lead to obesity. Social isolation leads to depression.

When YOU prioritize self-care, then you are able to embrace choices and maintain a positive attitude.

Control also matters. An **internal locus of control, called agency**, is what enables you to choose a positive attitude when useful. An internal locus of control leads to a sense of purpose, it helps you get out of the bed in the morning, or do meaningful work with a smile!

An **external locus of control** is everything else, those triggers that are beyond your control. If you repeatedly watch toxic messages on social media that perpetuate extremism, then you will be more likely to feel polarization or anxiety or depression. Too many of my clients have addictions (e.g., workaholism, digital, drugs, alcohol, sex) that prevent them from being their best self.

How YOU practice self-care varies greatly. But when you do, then you and your team will be more productive. There are many good TED videos and TED MED and YouTube videos that address self-care. Check them out!

Every Next Gen leader needs to become the change they wish to see!

YOU can practice gratitude, surround yourself with positivity, reframe challenges, and prioritize self-care. You can develop the behavior of expressing a positive attitude.

If you're doubtful, ask me about my PhD dissertation research! In conversation with one of my mentors, Marty Seligman, he said, *"The purpose of life is to discover your gifts, and the meaning of life is to give them away."*

You can spread positivity and inspire those around you on this exciting journey.

Related Books

Frederickson, B.L. (2009). *Positivity; Top-Notch Research Reveals the Upward Spiral That Will Change Your Life.* Three Rivers Press.

Friedman, S.E. (2013). *Family Business and Positive Psychology; New Planning Strategies for the 21st Century.* American Bar Association.

Gordon, J. (2008). *The Energy Bus: 10 Rules to Fuel Your Life, Work, and Team with Positive Energy.* Wiley.

Gray, D.W. (2018). Dissertation: *Positive Psychology Coaching Protocols; Creating Competitive Advantage for Leader Development.* Proquest: Ann Arbor, MI.

Luthans, F., Youssef-Morgan, C.M. & Avolio, B.J. (2007). *Psychological Capital; Developing the human competitive edge.* Oxford University Press; Oxford.

Luthans, F., Youssef-Morgan, C.M. & Avolio, B.J. (2015). *Psychological Capital and Beyond.* Oxford University Press; Oxford.

Seligman, M.E.P. (2011). *Flourish; A Visionary New Understanding of Happiness and Well-Being.* Atria; New York.

Seligman, M.E.P. (2018). *The Hope Circuit; A Psychologist's Journey From Helplessness to Optimism.* Public Affairs Books.

Chapter 2: The Family System

The top two key behaviors:
   3. Keep confidences about family business wealth.
   4. Handle family business disagreements in private.

"The secret to happiness is hiding on top of a mountain until your teenagers grow up and leave home!"

My Assumptions for the Family System:

1. Your elders have shared values, assumptions, behaviors that may be stated/ unstated
2. Your current family will change over time
3. How you communicate, make decisions, and address conflict can be improved
4. You need a safe process for assessing and developing the unique strengths of your key leaders

3. Keep confidences about family business wealth.

This is the MOST important behavior for **family members**, based on my research to date.

If you are a family member working in your business, then others may regard you with **both envy and fear**. They may envy your wealth or vacations. They may envy the fact that family members typically have more career clarity than non-family members. Assuming that you and your family members are competent workers, then you could spend your career working in a business or ownership capacity. And non-family leaders may fear family members for the same reasons.

Family members who are owners typically have a long term or multi-generational view of assets and investments. They keep confidences. They share wealth. **Virtually ALL philanthropy has been a gift from private owners.** Consider your local colleges, parks, symphonies, museums, or libraries. Consider how your family contributes to charity.

As soon as they can speak, young children need to practice keeping confidences about family wealth. Parents and family elders need to teach the importance of keeping secrets.

Social media guidelines are common for wealthy families, and more crucial than ever. You never want to attract thieves (when the main house is empty) or risk the safety of your loved ones (when traveling without escorts in remote locations). One of my clients posted photos on social media when he bought a new Porsche during a recession when they had to reduce jobs. His sister was furious!

Regardless of your wealth or financial capital, I strongly recommend that you adopt a social media guideline for your owners immediately.

Here are some comments from frustrated, lonely Next Gen leaders. Use these like warnings, and if you hear them, then YOU need to address those people immediately, in private.

"I get worried that my cousins will say the wrong thing about our family wealth. The content they post on social media is sensitive information, and they just seem to be clueless. We need a social media guideline immediately."

"I know that we have more assets than most in our community. But I never know who to talk to about that fact. So, I tend to clam up when someone asks about our family wealth."

Here are some practical suggestions for keeping confidences about wealth. Play with them a bit...

1. Understand the Importance of Confidentiality

Secrets shared are no longer confidential. That's why so many of my clients "keep it within the family." They know that information has its own weird energy, like gossip or investment tips.

My clients use guidelines to contain information. Some guidelines are "good to have" and some guidelines are "need to have" recommendations. Keeping confidences is more than a good practice. **Keeping confidentiality is a "need to have" requirement**!

Your family and non-family leaders need to know that keeping confidences about family business wealth is not just about trust, but it's also about preserving the integrity and stability of the business.

There is never an upside to talking about family wealth outside the family. Confidentiality builds a foundation of respect and fosters a sense of security among family members. Non-family members are loyal and often employed for decades because they are able to keep secrets.

Some of my clients do a confidential **annual assessment** of their long term employees and their senior leaders. YOU can create a spreadsheet and do this assessment in about 10 minutes. List your key people by name in the rows. The column headers can be 1) # years employed, 2) # direct reports, 3) # concerns or service complaints per year, 4) $ value of direct responsibilities, 5) $ current salary and compensation, 6) # years potential, 7) $ potential value ahead, 8) ability to live the values, including confidentiality, on a scale from 1-10. These are your confidential notes of performance tracking measures.

I often state, **"A little structure goes a long ways."** If you created that spreadsheet today, what would you learn?

Give it a few minutes. Play around a little bit...

2. Clearly Define Roles and Responsibilities

Information is a form of currency, just like a $100 bill or any capital asset. Information needs to be shared within the ownership team, according to mutually understood agreements.

I often use a **Decision Matrix** with clients to determine who needs Input (I), Responsibility (R) or Decision (D) on topics such as family employment guidelines or distributions. Sensitive financial information needs to be shared with the owners, and key executives such as the CEO and CFO. All leaders need to know how they contribute, and what topics are confidential.

Start by creating another simple spreadsheet for your Decision Matrix. The rows can include 20+ possible decisions, such as "Determining criteria for ownership" or "Philanthropy" or "Leadership compensation." The columns typically include "Family or Family Council" "Owners" "Board" or "Management." Every one of my clients has their own reasons for determining who should have Input (I), Responsibility (R) or Decision (D) for those decisions.

A second project management model that clearly defines roles is the **RACI Matrix**. Think of it as a simple project responsibility assignment chart to map out key tasks and milestones. Use a whiteboard or spreadsheet. The key tasks are listed in the rows. The columns define who is Responsible, Accountable, Consulted or Informed on that key task.

YOU need clear guidelines and expectations about those roles. Spend 20 minutes and develop your Decision Matrix or RACI Matrix. A little structure goes a long ways toward better governance!

I often ask clients to complete the Decision Matrix as individuals, then bring their notes to the Family Meeting. That makes for a lively discussion! Then YOU may need to review or update your Decision Matrix every 3-4 years.

You need **access to valid information**. One of my CFO clients occasionally asked different teams to provide financial summaries of the same project. The project managers thought it was a waste of time or a test of their ability to maximize productivity. It was both, and it was more than that! The CFO used that tactic to determine if financial information flowed to him consistently, or if there were gaps in their reporting structures. He always found gaps.

And YOU need **to protect confidentiality.** Cybersecurity is a scary example of real threats that are gaining sophistication. The losses are significant. Family-owned businesses are targets for criminals because you may not have rigorous security protocols to protect your wealth and mange business transactions.

In the last few months I have heard five examples of $1M losses, sometimes from the same client business. The FBI, insurance vendors, and bank partners cannot protect confidentiality, they can only react. Owners like you need to develop ongoing, rigorous security protocols to protect your wealth.

Bottom line: **there is never a time when it is acceptable or smart to boast about family wealth.**

3. Implement Secure Communication Channels

Owners and executives will always need secure communication channels to share and discuss sensitive financial information.

That fact requires that YOU **invest in secure technology**, such as encrypted messaging platforms or dedicated secure servers that can minimize the risk of unauthorized access to your confidential data. You can get started today. The rewards and risks are huge.

One vendor told me that cybersecurity insurance increased over 700% in 2023.

I asked, "Was that adequate?"

And he said, "No. Never."

Your G1 family business leaders may have met around a kitchen table or work table. **Now, whether you are G1 or G5 or a non-family leader, you need to meet around a secure digital table.**

All of my clients use digital systems to exchange information and transfer money. Every financial market now processes those assets in micro-seconds to gain margins and make money. The result of international banking and ISO financial transaction protocols is that most transactions are safer than ever. Thank goodness!

I can recall traveling in Europe and Mexico with cash or American Express paper checks. Now I use bank transfers to pay vendors anywhere. We all do so.

How secure and confidential are your documents? Here are two resources from two expert friends. For family documents such as capital and financial assets, or the favorite veterinarian, I recommend Josh Kanter's platform at Leafplanner. For confidential board meeting document exchange, including minutes and strategic planning, I recommend Charles Glick's platform called Foresight at Board-Ops. You can develop more secure communication channels today.

We all need to make secure decisions about assets and strategy. You may use a Zoom AI summary of talking points. Or you may never do so, because you want confidentiality or handwritten notes locked in a security box every night.

I predict that cybersecurity will continue to be a critical investment for your family enterprises. **The pace of technology is slower today than it will ever be in the future.** (See the books listed below by Kurzweil or Diamandis.)

4. Educate and Train Family Members

One of the best reasons for regular family meetings is to share information with your loved ones.

For many years I have shared a list of 50 or more **"What if…?" scenarios** for people to consider. For instance, "What if one of the business owners has a severe accident and is not able to work for 6 months?" or "What if the previous generation has transferred ownership but "talks too much in meetings" or "fears that the kids will make mistakes or screw things up"?

One of the most frequent "What if…?" scenarios addresses conflict and confidentiality in family meetings. What do you do when family members have different perspectives, or accelerate conflict, during a meeting with outside advisors (attorneys, wealth advisors, or business consultants like me)? My experience is that everyone in that meeting needs to decrease task conflict, improve communication, and protect confidentiality.

YOU can provide education and training to family members on the importance of confidentiality.

YOU can share examples and case studies that highlight the potential consequences of breaching confidentiality.

Those "What if…? discussions will help reinforce the understanding that protecting the family business wealth is a shared responsibility.

The rule of the 5 P's is simple: **Prior Planning Prevents Poor Performance.** Maybe that could be another Postix reminder for you?

5. Regularly Review and Update Privacy Policies

What do you do if a family member buys a new home, and shares photos of their catered poolside party with celebrities?

You may have a social media policy that discourages such posts, because that new home is an obvious targets for thieves. In places where kidnapping and ransom demands are common, privacy policies are a requirement.

You need to stay up to date on privacy regulations and ensure that your family business has robust privacy policies in place. As technology and cyber threats increase, you will need to regularly review and update these policies to adapt to your changing circumstances and those emerging risks.

Most of my clients have a social media guideline such as "Never post anything that could cause harm or risk to any family member."

You may want to contribute to charity anonymously, rather than use your family foundation name.

You may want to require digital spyware and encryption practices as a requirement for protecting your wealth.

Keeping confidences about family wealth is a choice. The result is crucial for maintaining trust, family stability, and the long-term success of your business.

YOU need to reinforce this behavior.

To repeat once again, **there is no upside to sharing confidences about family wealth!**

I sure hope that you get this point! Repetition never hurts. Repetition never hurts...

Related Books

Diamandis, P.H., & Kotler, S. (2012). *Abundance; The Future Is Better Than You Think (Exponential Technology Series).* Free Press.

Diamandis, P. & Kotler, S. (2020). *The Future is Faster Than You Think; How Converging Technologies Are Transforming Business, Industries, and Our Lives.* Simon & Schuster.

Kurzweil, R. (2006). *The Singularity is Near: When Humans Transcend Biology.* Penguin.

Kurzweil, R. (2013). *How to Create a Mind; The Secret of Human Thought Revealed.* Penguin.

Rhodes, K. & Lansky, D. (2013). *Managing Conflict in the Family Business: Understanding Challenges at the Interchapter of Family and Business.* Palgrave Macmillan, New York. Part of the Family Business Consulting Group Series.

Ward, J. (2004). *Perpetuating the Family Business; 50 Lessons Learned from Long-Lasting, Successful Families in Business.* Palgrave.

Wells, D. (2020). *When Anything Is Possible; Wealth and the Art of Strategic Living.* Self-published.

4. Handle family business disagreements in private.

This is one of the MOST important behaviors for **family members**, based on my research to date.

You have probably heard the saying "blood is thicker than water" as a way to describe the strong ties of family kinship.

From tribal clans to divorce courts, the "**Honor Code**" is an ancient way to protect those strong kinship ties, in every culture, in every corner of the world.

People have always fought to protect the shared assets and integrity of family.

There is a **sacred understanding that disagreements within a family should be discussed in private**, behind closed doors. If anyone breaks that behavior, then the family ties are weakened and conflicts escalate.

Here are some comments from frustrated Family Business leaders. Use these as triggers. If you hear one of these comments, or if you state one of them, then YOU need to get some help, in a private location.

"I worry about the impact that public disagreements can have on our family's reputation and the overall stability of our business. I need strategies to manage conflicts privately and effectively."

"Disagreements are exhausting. I need to avoid them, but my family likes to create conflicts, especially on the warehouse floor or the office lobby. It gets noisy."

Here are some suggestions for how YOU can handle family business disagreements in private.

Try them... they work well!

1. Create a Safe and Confidential Space

Family members need to meet behind closed doors, and they need to respect confidentiality agreements.

When I recently facilitated a Next Gen family meeting, their "check in activity" included personal and professional updates on a scale of 1-10, plus examples. **Then each person stated if they had any concerns about confidentiality breaches, from themselves or from anyone else.**

One result of that opening activity was that it grounded everyone, modeled trust, and enabled them to discuss difficult topics. Try it at your next family meeting!

All family members need to feel comfortable discussing disagreements privately. YOU can emphasize the importance of confidentiality and ensure that everyone understands that sensitive discussions should stay within the family circle.

There is a sacred boundary within strong families, and that boundary needs to be preserved.

When consulting Next Gen leaders, I often help them identify shared key values, develop a constitution or charter, ground rules for confidentiality, and facilitate regular family meetings.

2. Foster Open and Honest Communication

Open communication happens when those who have concerns share their concerns directly. That's the rule. Here are some more good rules for open communication.

Gossip cannot be tolerated. Period. Just as "loose lips sink ships," gossip kills trust. And all people gossip at times. We gossip when we explore ideas, like "I heard a rumor that…" or "Did you hear…?" If you are inclined to gossip, then others will imitate your behavior. And you will soon be the subject of the next rumor. That's why YOU should never perpetuate gossip.

Triangulation (when Bill needs to talk to his sister Sarah but instead talks to his cousin Matt) cannot be tolerated. Triangulation always leads to conflict. That's why triangulation cannot be tolerated. You need to make direct communication the rule by modeling open dialogue, emphasizing the importance of active listening and empathy. When you hear someone start to triangulate, you need to cut them off and state, "We don't tolerate triangulation in our business."

Active listening requires that YOU seek to understand, repeat your understanding, and then correct your summary until the other person feels validated. The phrase "I see you and understand you" is a requirement for safety (physical, emotional, professional, psychological). If you have never said, "I see you and understand you" to a loved one, then try it today. It works well!

Empathy is defined as understanding another person's perspective. Thankfully, empathy is a behavior that can be developed and taught. Parents can develop empathy in children. Teachers, especially those who use fictional stories, can develop empathy in their students. Business leaders who listen to their customers can develop empathy.

You can create an environment where everyone feels heard and valued, allowing for the expression of diverse perspectives and opinions.

Honest communication may help prevent disagreements from escalating and should promote productive problem-solving.

Good communication is a critical skill that can be taught, reinforced and rewarded in all family enterprises.

3. Set Ground Rules for Conflict Management

Conflict can be defined as a response to different perspectives. We all have different perspectives. That fact implies that if there are nine billion people on the planet, then there are over nine billion different possibilities for conflict. Yikes!

Task conflict is good, because it often leads to innovation. When owners discuss the strengths and weaknesses of a CEO or senior leader, they should have some task conflict. When new ideas are applied to any team or organization, that is called innovation. All teams need to adapt and overcome!

However, **relationship conflict** is bad, because it perpetuates negative judgements. If Nancy hates her cousin Jean, and they vent in front of others, that behavior needs to be stopped. Immediately.

One of my clients needed to accelerate succession planning because two of their Next Gen leaders had a habit of verbally fighting in front of others. One leader was family. One leader was like family. And they fought since they were children, for over 20 years. They didn't know that their relationship conflict prevented them from working together. No one had been able to get them to stop! I conducted 360 leadership assessments for each of them, and they learned what behaviors to start doing, stop doing, or continue doing. Their results were profound- one of my best succession planning success stories!

Thankfully, you have many choices when facing conflicts. YOU can choose to be more **assertive** (of your own perspective). Or you can choose to be more **cooperative** (of others' perspectives.)

When someone insults you, then you have **five responses** to consider when responding to that negative stimulus. You can choose to **avoid, accommodate, compete, collaborate or adopt consensus** when responding to others. I often use the model from Thomas-Kilman to describe those five responses, do role plays, and practice new respectful behaviors.

If you are inclined to respond in a certain manner— such as avoiding your uncle when he argues for political opinions that you don't share— try accommodating him by asking him to explain his opinions. That's an example of **conflict management, when you respond to others so that you can manage your response.**

"**Conflict resolution**" is an overused phrase cited by therapists, who want a clear process for minimizing conflicts. "**Conflict transformation**" is another aspirational phrase that tends to muddy the water. I avoid those phrases because they don't describe what works.

"Managing Conflict" is a more accurate description of what we do regularly.

Here is another success story. For nine years I directed a non-profit summer camp program at a Quaker School near Washington, D.C. We grew 800% because we were all focused on the safety of children. Our team of 150 adults served thousands of families and Next Gen leaders.

Did you know that most Quaker communities use a process to identify and reduce conflict? Throughout history, Quakers fight for women's rights, social justice, peace activism, business integrity, and non-violent communication. Imagine a "Silent Meeting" with several hundred high-school aged students and adults sitting in benches that face each other, until someone feels called to stand and speak.

One activity used to help you center "into the moment of spirit" is to imagine a glass jar with muddy water. As the mud settles to the bottom of the jar, **YOU can imagine centering into your core values so that you can respond to conflict with clarity.**

Quakers believe that consensus is possible for any group. The process requires identifying shared values, common guidelines, and including all voices in decision making.

You can establish guidelines for managing conflict. Here is a short list of guidelines (repeated from chapter 1) that I have used for decades. Add your guidelines to this list so that you can minimize relationship conflict.

> Be here now
> Assume positive intent in others
> Listen to understand
> Provide honest feedback
> Celebrate what works
> Keep our humor
> Add your guidelines...

You may include setting boundaries on behavior, establishing a neutral mediator, or implementing structured conflict management techniques. Try some of these tactics. Then edit them at any time.

Task conflict is necessary and often leads to innovation, particularly when you adopt ground rules and manage your responses.

4. Seek External Mediation if Necessary

In my youth, I played ice hockey and worked as a referee for many years. I joke that those years were good opportunities to learn how to break up fights— certainly a transferable skill when working with people in conflict!

A better opportunity was tremendous role modeling from my parents, who expected me "to work out conflict with my younger siblings." At one point we were encouraged to wrestle in the basement.

At other points we were encouraged to go for a walk and talk together. Throughout history people have often worked out conflicts by talking and walking together. At Stanford's School of Business they encourage "twalking." Try that activity with someone and notice what happens!

Family business disagreements can certainly become complex and emotionally charged.

I recall once standing in front of the door when a furious Next Gen leader wanted to charge out of the room. His siblings, parents and grandmother wanted him to stay and discuss the situation. I literally "stood in the way" (another phrase used by the Quakers). I'm not sure if I'd ever do that again!

In emotionally charged cases like that example, you may need to work with an external mediator.

A neutral third party can provide a more objective perspective, facilitate productive discussions, and help find mutually beneficial solutions.

Lawyers are not typically skilled in mediation, and they are compensated in more billable hours if conflicts perpetuate. Accountants and wealth advisors are not skilled in mediation, and they benefit directly if there is a financial investment.

Instead, for expert mediators, see any of my colleagues at The Family Business Consulting Group, www.theFBCG.com.

5. Learn from Past Disagreements

There are countless stories of feuds or disagreements that are perpetuated over time, and over multiple generations.

One theory of family therapy adopts the belief that unresolved conflicts, especially between three people, need to be identified before family members can learn to collaborate. That approach presumes that people are broken and need to be fixed.

I prefer the positive psychology approach which assumes that **you can flourish,** especially when YOU learn lessons from the past.

Resilience is a behavior that can be measured and taught and developed. One measure of leadership success is the ability to "get up when you're punched in the gut." Those who overcome adversity are usually tremendous leaders because they have developed character skills. My experience is that most people have the hidden potential to be a better leader or manager. All YOU need is to learn from some adversity.

Resilience can be developed. For ten seasons, I led wilderness Outward Bound courses designed to help potential leaders develop essential skills like resilience and self-reliance and compassion. People who had never had the opportunity to practice leadership became experts at travelling in an unfamiliar environment. The terrain always varied- from sailing off the coast of Maine to canoeing through Minnesota, from caving in England to service projects in Boston Harbor, from dog-sledding in Ontario to ice climbing in New Hampshire. The course lengths also varied- from 24 days of backpacking and rock climbing to corporate 1-day programs.

Each course design included unfamiliar challenges. We assigned roles and rotated them daily. We taught skills like cooking or how to navigate using a map and a compass. We all learned to let other people lead. And every evening, we would circle up before dinner. Someone would read an inspirational quotation about leadership. And after dinner we would debrief the day by talking about "roses and thorns"- the good and the bad, the pluses and deltas. The results were astounding. On 100% of those courses strangers became leaders—people practiced resilience.

YOU don't need a wilderness expedition! You can encourage a culture of learning and growth immediately.

You can identify lessons learned, after any emotional conflict, take the time to **evaluate the situation and identify areas for improvement.**

Your team can use those experiences as opportunities to improve communication, strengthen relationships, and develop strategies to prevent similar conflicts in the future.

If Uncle Charles was cruel 20 years ago, there is no logical reason to assume that he will be cruel again. Or that his children will become cruel.

Discretion always matters.

When you handle family business disagreements in private, YOU need to practice effective communication, provide a safe space for dialogue, and a commitment to growth. Good managers make space, control pace, and practice grace.

When YOU implement these strategies and seek support, then YOU can navigate conflicts with grace and preserve harmony within your family and your business.

Related Books

Baron, J. & Lachenauer, R. (2021). *Harvard Business Review Family Business Handbook; How to Build and Sustain a Successful, Enduring Enterprise.* Harvard Business School Press.

Baumoel, D. & Trippe, B. (2016). *Deconstructing Conflict; Understanding Family Business, Shared Wealth and Power.* Continuity Media.

Friedman, S. (1998). *The Successful family Business.* Upstart Publishing.

Grant, A. (2023). *Hidden Potential; The Science of Achieving Greater Things.* Viking.

Lederach, J.P. (2003). *The Little Book of Conflict Transformation; Clear Articulation of the Guiding Principles By a Pioneer in the Field.* Good Books

Rhodes, K. & Lansky, D. (2013). *Managing Conflict in the Family Business: Understanding Challenges at the Interchapter of Family and Business.* Palgrave Macmillan, New York. Part of the Family Business Consulting Group Series.

Walsh, F. (2016). *Strengthening Family Resilience, 3rd Ed.* Guilford Press.

CHAPTER 3: THE BUSINESS SYSTEM

The top two key behaviors
- 5. **Measure business performance.**
- 6. **Use financial data to make decisions.**

My Assumptions for the Business System:

1. Your global, networked market demands will increase in complexity
2. Your technology-based solutions will define your success
3. Your working teams are the fundamental units in all successful businesses
4. Great managers maximize the productivity and profitability of others

5. Measure business performance.

This is the MOST important behavior for **business leaders**, based on my research to date.

All of my clients measure business performance. Some do a better job than others, because they **use data to identify more specific details**. They have learned to ask better questions, such as, "Which store sold the most widgets last week?" or "Did that sales increase result from a marketing campaign or discount?"

Most of my clients have weekly progress meetings to review key measures, like inventory, sales, cash on hand, production, efficiency, safety, quality.

The business maxim is "What gets measured leads to results." My corollary is, "**If you can't measure it, then it doesn't exist**."

Here are some comments from frustrated Next Gen Family Business leaders. Use these comments as "red flags" or "yellow flags." If you hear them, then use these comments as a trigger to have a conversation with someone. Today!

"I often feel frustrated. I know that I'm supposed to measure what matters, but I don't know how to get accurate numbers. I need strategies and tools to help me track key metrics and make informed decisions based on data."

"I just don't know how to evaluate the performance of my business accurately. I wish I knew how to establish a performance measurement system that aligns with our goals and objectives."

Here are some great tips that YOU can implement immediately. Try them!

1. Set clear and measurable goals

Humans have always "looked to the stars" with aspirational goals.

A familiar example is, "By the end of this decade we will land a man on the moon, and return him safely to earth." That moonshot, led by U.S. President John Kennedy, Jr., was buttressed by a 3.2% budget allocation from the U.S. congress to create the National Aeronautics and Space Association (NASA).

When YOU set clear and specific goals for your business, then you are more likely to have success. **Aspirational goals** are big, and may not be attainable.

Operational goals are necessary for your success. You may have an aspirational goal to eliminate the wealth disparity in your state within a decade. And you may have an operational goal to increase your charitable giving to feed at least 1,000 people per year in your state.

Those goals should be measurable and aligned with your overall business strategy.

Many of my clients actively contribute to charity using specific goals. I often ask, "**What charitable interest do you want to support?**" That discussion informs philanthropy, and often serves as a lever to accelerate family capital.

When you have well-defined objectives, then you can track your progress and evaluate your performance accurately.

2. Identify key performance indicators (KPIs) and Objectives and Key Results (OKRs)

Today, there are two dominant approaches to measuring goals in organizations.

The first approach, **Key Performance Indicators (KPIs)**, is a top-down approach written by business managers in support of the owner's strategy.

The second approach, **Objectives and Key Results (OKRs)** are written by the individuals and support the strategy of the managers and workers. Typically, when writing OKRs, people write three main objectives every quarter, WHAT they need to focus on. Then they write three key results to measure HOW they will achieve those objectives.

Each system can work well in a family-owned business. KPIs are commonly used in manufacturing where outputs are defined from managers and product limitations (like robots or work hours). OKRs are commonly used with technology or independent workers who expect to define their focus and outcomes. (See details in my *OKR Leadership* book cited below).

YOU can start by **determining the key metrics** that are most relevant to your business's success. Your KPIs and OKRs will vary depending on your industry, and they should reflect critical aspects such as sales growth, profitability, customer satisfaction, and employee productivity.

Many of my clients focus on three metrics: people, process and technology.

Leaders like you can regularly monitor your KPIs and OKRs to gauge your team's performance.

3. **Implement a performance measurement system**

   Athletes are expert at measuring their training in preparation for a competition. Same with great musicians, investors, authors, and business leaders like you.

   The steps are simple. **Start with a baseline,** where YOU are now. Then establish a **system to track and measure** performance consistency. That's all you need!

   There are so many free and low cost software resources available today, and so many experts in using them, that you have no excuse! Consider Slack, Asana, Microsoft Excel, QuickBooks, Microsoft Project, Salesforce, or whatever cousin Bob recommends...

   You can hire someone from Upwork or Fiverr or your local chamber of commerce. Make it easy to use. Select something that looks cool, because data visualization increases usage. Your performance management system could include colorful performance dashboards, real time updates, financial reporting systems, or project management tools.

I often state, "**A little structure goes a long ways.**" By having a structured approach to measurement, you can gather accurate data and make informed decisions.

4. Conduct regular performance reviews

When you visit a physician, a nurse checks your vital signs like weight, heart rate, blood pressure, and adds that data to your confidential health records.

Most of my clients do a similar "check in" every month or every quarter to assess how the business is doing. This is a behavior that YOU can implement today.

The process is simple. **Start with whatever metrics** you currently have. Then **schedule regular performance reviews to assess your progress** towards your business goals. These reviews can be conducted on a monthly, quarterly, or annual basis, depending on the nature of your business.

There's no mystery or secret sauce involved. Try it!

Business leaders use numbers ALL the time.

Data is described as either **quantitative** (using numbers) or **qualitative** (using images or words). You can also add qualitative data, such as client stories, referrals, anecdotes, word clouds, photos from Instagram or Facebook or LinkedIn from clients.

The **main point is to use the quantitative and qualitative data available today** so that you can use those performance reviews as an opportunity to identify strengths, weaknesses, and areas for improvement.

Look for trends. Celebrate surprises !%$

Play around a little bit 😊

Every sporting event has a scoreboard, timer, and rules. Why would you avoid measures in your family business?

Playing football, just like your business, requires setting clear goals, identifying key performance indicators, implementing a performance measurement system, and conducting regular performance reviews.

Family Business leaders like you can gain valuable insights into your business' performance and increase effective decision-making.

Don't wait to develop this behavior! Play with these tactics...

Related Books

Doerr, J. (2018). *Measure What Matters; How Google, Bono and the Gates Foundation Rock the World with OKRs.* Penguin.

Gray, D. (2019). *Objectives + Key Results (OKR) Leadership; How to Apply Silicon Valley's Secret Sauce to Your Career, Team or Organization.* Gray Publications.

Harms, T. (2018). *The 12 Questions that Keep Family Business Directors Awake at Night.* Mercer Capital.

LaMorte, B. (2022). *The OKRs Field Book; A Step-by-Step Guide for Objectives and Key Results Coaches.* Wiley.

McNeill, M (2020). *The Prosperity Playbook; Planning for a Successful Family Business Succession.* Redwood.

Schmeider, J. (2014). *Innovation in the Family Business; Succeeding Through Generations.* Palgrave. Part of the Family Business Publication Series.

6. Use financial data to make decisions.

This is one of the MOST important behavior for **business leaders**, based on my research to date.

Most business leaders use financial data to make decisions, because they must do so.

You may be good at using financial data. **You need to become great at using financial data.** With most of my clients, financial literacy is a skill gap that needs to be developed.

Here are some comments from frustrated Next Gen Family Business leaders. Use these comments as "red flags" or "yellow flags." If you hear them, then use these comments as a trigger to have a conversation with someone. Today!

"I often feel overwhelmed by the numbers and financial jargon. It can be challenging to make informed decisions when I feel like I'm drowning in spreadsheets and reports."

"As a non-financially inclined person, I often feel isolated. I just don't know how to use financial data to drive business *decisions. I went on YouTube last night to do some research, but I need more resources that are specific to our business."*

Here are some tactics to help YOU develop your financial decision making behavior. Play with them a bit...

1. Develop financial literacy

I often state, **"Action leads to learning. If you're not taking action, then you're not learning."**

You can educate yourself on financial concepts and terminology.

There are only two approaches to adult learning: formal and informal. **Formal learning** is defined as the content or coursework required to demonstrate mastery of a skill, like the competency tests for becoming a Certified Public Accountant.

Informal learning is what most adults do to master a skill or competency, just in time, using available resources. You can ask your CFO, or Uncle Dan, or a board member to teach you a skill.

You can click on a YouTube video, or ask for help from your local Family Business Center, your board, a Certified Public Accountant (CPA), or Certified Financial Planner (CFP), Registered Investment Advisor (RIA) or your Family Office.

You can create a digital library with definitions and examples of basic terms such as balance sheets, income statements, and cash flow statements.

You can volunteer to serve on the finance committee of a local board.

You can join an investment club.

You can subscribe to online courses from Family Business Centers, or Multi Family Offices like The Life Academy, or webinars and courses from The Family Business Consulting Group. There are literally hundreds of educational programs and resources that can help you develop your financial literacy.

Note the long list of books below! One of my clients created a book discussion group, using books or any YouTube video summary, and hosts monthly 30-minute discussions on financial matters. You can assign others to lead those monthly discussions so that YOU model financial literacy learning.

2. Collaborate with financial experts

We all require expertise. Don't hesitate to seek the expertise of expert financial professionals, like your accountants or financial advisors. They can provide valuable insights and guidance on interpreting financial data and making informed decisions.

Many of my clients with over $1M in investable assets have **multiple financial advisors so that they get multiple perspectives.**

Many leaders of small family businesses **talk to multiple accountants and wealth advisors every year**, so that they get multiple perspectives.

It's a small investment in time and energy, and can lead to significant rewards.

You can encourage your youngest family members to practice saving, investing and giving so that they can develop those skills as they age.

You can invite family members to observe board meetings so that they can observe how financial data informs decision making.

You can use three jars to teach children the need to invest 1/3, and save 1/3 before spending 1/3 of your assets.

You can share any of the great books cited below.

3. Set clear financial goals

Too many people do not have written financial goals, which limits their potential. I've been an executive coach for dozens of wealth advisors, since 1997, and to my surprise, **they are not required to have their own financial goals.** They are compensated based on how much others invest in their products and services. A wealth advisor from Wells Fargo or Ameriprise will get up to 4% trailing earnings over time from whatever investments their clients make. Those advisors with more assets under management (AUM) are recognized in *Forbes* or the Million Dollar Round Table (MDRT). That system rewards their financial management goals. But it does not reward their clients, like you or me.

Your financial goals can be described in a similar way. I write annual and quarterly financial objectives, that align with my overall business strategy. I post them on the office door in my home so that my adult children can track how I am progressing toward those financial goals.

You can do the same.

Start by writing goals that are SMART—specific, measurable, attainable, realistic, and time-bound. Then you can monitor your progress and make data-driven decisions to achieve those goals.

Most of my clients share their financial goals with the ownership group or with their executive managers.

Many boards require managers to share their financial and operational goals.

Transparency in financial goals is a trend that is likely to continue, with digital access to information. If your financial goals can be shared broadly (as percentage increases or decreases, not as raw numbers) then some employees (of any age, but especially Millennials and Gen Z) may become more engaged in achieving those financial goals.

Many of my clients share percent-to-goal numbers monthly or quarterly, and reward milestones.

Note that **all** of the books listed below focus on setting clear financial goals. You can select a book and share your financial goals today. Just pick one!

4. Implement financial tracking systems

The myth is that we are working harder than ever, using technology to respond faster to more complexity than ever.

The reality is that today is the slowest, simplest work pace that YOU will ever experience. For the rest of your life!

You are expert at embracing new innovations and technology, using your prefrontal cortex. And you are a fear-based creature who avoids innovation, using the oldest part of your brain.

You can no longer resist the need to use technology and software solutions to track and analyze your financial data effectively.

Fact: Digital systems are more accurate and efficient than paper systems.

Artificial Intelligence (AI) already processes most of the financial transactions in global business, in nanoseconds. Artificial Generalized Intelligence (AGI) or Artificial Super Intelligence (ASI) may soon provide financial recommendations that out-perform any market or combined human knowledge, in nanoseconds.

When you implement more robust accounting systems and financial management tools, you can streamline your decision-making process and provide real-time insights into your business's financial health. Internal accounting tools are inexpensive and can be customized for your business sector, or they can be generic such as QuickBooks.

Organizations mature, just like individuals mature.

I often state, "**Verbal** agreements helped the founders. **Written** agreements accelerate growth. **Digital processes** define the probability of your future success."

In addition to your internal reporting and reporting cadence, make sure that you have regular **external audits** from qualified financial and legal experts in your sector to assess and recommend how to reduce taxes, increase profits, manage risks, consider liquidity.

The largest operating expense for most of my clients is talent.

Look at your profit and loss statements. Your investment in your **employees and compensation is likely 40-60% of your revenue, and 100% discretionary.**

How do you know who to keep, and who to let go from your workforce? I'm often hired to assess the talent capability of family business leaders, using the 360

Leadership Development Consulting Process I developed. You may need to assess your key leaders, develop a succession plan, and **audit your talent** immediately. For details see www.AssessNextGen.com

For financial and legal audits, see the books listed below for vendors and software recommendations.

Developing the ability to use financial data to make decisions takes time and effort. By following these tips and leveraging the expertise of financial professionals, YOU can enhance your financial acumen and make more informed business decisions.

This behavior, using financial data to make decisions, is critical for your business success.

Numbers drive businesses. Get started today!

Related Books

Aronoff, C., McClure, S. & Ward, J. (2011, 3rd ed.) *Family Business Compensation.* Palgrave MacMillan, New York. Part of the Family Business Consulting Group Series.

Beman, K., Kinght, J. (2006). *Financial Intelligence; A Manager's Guide to Knowing What the Numbers Really Mean.* Harvard Business School Press.

Finance for Managers (2002). Harvard Business Essentials Series. Cambridge, MA.

Grubman, J. (2013). *Strangers in Paradise; How Families Adapt to Wealth Across Generations.* Self-published.

Grubman, J., Jaffe, D.T. & Keffeler, K. (2023). *Wealth 3.0; The Future of Wealth Advising.* Self-published.

Housel, M. (2020). *The Psychology of Money; Timeless lessons on wealth, greed and happiness.* Harriman House; New York.

Lansky, D. (2016). *Family Wealth Continuity; Building a Foundation for the Future*. A Family Business Publication.

Pendergast, J., Ward, J. & Brun de Pontet, S. (2011). *Building a Successful family Business Board; A Guide for Leaders, Directors, and Families.* Palgrave Macmillan; the Family Business Consulting Group Series. New York.

Robbins, T. (2016). *MONEY Master the Game; 7 Simple Steps to Financial Freedom*. Simon & Schuster

Robbins, T. (2017). *Unshakeable; Your Financial Freedom Playbook Creating Peace of Mind in a World of Volatility.* Simon & Schuster.

Twist, L. (2017, 2nd ed). *The Soul of Money; Transforming Your Relationship With Money and Life.* Norton.

Chapter 4: The Learning System

The top two key behaviors in the learning system:
7. Reward employees who provide outstanding service.
8. Provide performance feedback for your direct reports and teams.

"I'm looking for a mentor who can show me how to get rich without boring me with a lot of advice."

My Assumptions for the Learning System:

1. Your curiosity is innate and can be nurtured
2. Practicing personal mastery is the cornerstone of your learning organization
3. Your mental models are like videos of your potential
4. Great leaders co-create a shared vision of a better future

7. Reward employees who provide outstanding service.

This is the MOST important behavior for **adult learners**, based on my research to date.

Did you know that Family Business employees typically report higher employee engagement scores than employees at publicly-owned companies?

Engagement is a measure of how connected people feel toward their work and toward others. For over 40 years the engagement level of publicly-owned companies has plateaued at only 30%, which explains why so many people are actively looking for a different employer!

Loyalty matters for owners, customers, and for employees. In fact, rewarding employees who provide outstanding service is one of the behaviors that **describes most successful family-owned businesses.**

How about your business? How many employees have been with your business for more than 10 years? 20 years? 30 years? **Longevity is important. But, service is more important.**

How do you know who provides outstanding service? And how do you reward those people?

Here are some comments from frustrated Family Business leaders. Use these comments as "red flags" or "yellow flags." If you hear them, then use these comments as a trigger to have a conversation with someone. Today.

"I often feel underappreciated for the extra effort I put into my work. It would be great to be recognized and rewarded... somehow."

"I see my colleagues providing outstanding service, but their efforts usually go unnoticed. It's disheartening and makes me question if my efforts will be valued as well."

"I believe recognizing outstanding service should be a priority. It not only boosts morale but also encourages employees to continue delivering exceptional results. We need to change some incentives around here."

Here are some proven tactics that are not expensive, and reward desired behaviors such as outstanding service. Play with them... they work well!

1. Create a Culture of Recognition

The first step is YOU have to identify your desired behaviors. That's why vision statements, value statements, job descriptions and behavior performances need to be written and shared.

Verbal assumptions just don't work over generations! Once those desired behaviors are written, then you can foster a culture where recognizing and rewarding outstanding service becomes part of your organization's DNA.

Recognition is quick and easy.

Many of my clients ask, "Who has been outstanding this week?" They seek to identify people at all levels, then they recognize those outstanding employees publicly.

You may know that **public recognition is a bigger motivator of desired behaviors than cash.** Monetary rewards are important, and people are more motivated by "carrots than sticks." Consider those who work after hours, or who push to complete a project under budget or before a deadline. What motivates them? What motivates you? One consistent theme in 100+ years of social psychology research is that we are social animals. Public recognition is the best way to validate and reward desired behaviors, like quality standards, safety minimums, or outstanding customer service.

You can start every meeting with, "Who has an uplifting example of our values?"

The deepest human yearning is to be seen positively.

We all want positive regard at three levels: 1) **safety** (physical, emotional, psychological, professional), 2) **connections** (direct and virtual and hybrid), and 3) **dignity** (respect for each individual).

And the currency of positive regard is attention, which costs 5 seconds and lasts for a career!

One of my clients is so skilled at public recognition that he cannot walk through a warehouse quickly, because he stops to connect with so many people.

You can celebrate outstanding service with success stories at the start of every meeting, shout-outs during team meetings, internal newsletters, testimonial sharing, or a dedicated recognition program with virtual points.

2. Tailor Rewards to Individuals

Every good manager knows that rewards need to match the motivations of others. But you may not know how to assess and match others.

Here is a great activity I've used for decades that will help you.

Create a simple chart with 4 columns. Column one is a list of 5-6 important people in your world. They may be important because of your **relationship** (like a partner or child) or their **results** (like a colleague or vendor). Column two is a list of what each of those important people value (e.g., money, recognition, promotion, autonomy, structure, etc.) Column three is a list of what YOU should say or do. Finally, column 4 is a list of what YOU should NOT say or do. This process, called **Value-Based Coaching**, is one way to make sure that YOU are matching the motivations of others. Keep the list confidential, and look at it when coaching others.

If you don't know what those important people value, then you need to spend time with them and observe what they say or do.

Behavior always screams louder than words!

People like different rewards, such as a bonus, a promotion, additional time off, or a heartfelt thank-you note. The key is for you to make the reward meaningful and personalized for them.

3. Provide Growth Opportunities

Throughout history, workers have been objectified as "hands and feet" or managed as if they were an expensive "resource" like a machine.

Most of the organizational management "science" tried to increase returns with decreased investments, for owners who maximized productivity. Yes, those trends have always existed in closely-held enterprises, from plantations to factories. But none of my clients are cruel capitalists.

My clients care about their organizations and they want to help people flourish. Like a gardener who works with the soil nearby to develop flourishing plants, YOU can help people flourish. We all have talents. Your challenge is to accelerate the hidden potential in others, so that they can excel.

There are two ways to describe behaviors in your organization.

Operational behaviors are what people do every day to get the job done. These behaviors need to be done efficiently, to "keep the lights on" or "deliver products on time."

Aspirational behaviors are the exceptional, remarkable behaviors that people do to exceed expectations. These behaviors are so remarkable that people remark about your quality product or service. They provide unsolicited referrals. They encourage friends to work with your team. They suggest innovations.

Managers, by definition, need to maximize the productivity of others.

You will need to identify both types of behaviors, and reward both operational and aspirational behaviors.

You will always need people to do the operational behaviors.

And you will always want to encourage people to do something outstanding, something aspirational.

Those are called **"Growth Opportunities" because people need to be encouraged to stretch into new desired behaviors.** Ambitious, goal-driven people need to know that they are encouraged to do something outstanding.

You can provide growth opportunities such as additional responsibilities, stretch assignments, cross functional projects, access to board members or mentorship opportunities.

Most of these examples do NOT require any additional expenses, just your encouragement and introductions. Give it a try!

4. Encourage Peer Recognition

Teams are much more effective at fostering innovation and celebrating outstanding service than any one manager or one owner.

I often state, **"Teams win. Individuals flounder."**

Many of my clients have a virtual point system to recognize outstanding service. If each employee has up to 50 virtual points to distribute every month, then they can list another person and their outstanding behavior on a spreadsheet… and everyone can track the leaderboard.

At the end of the quarter or end of the year, those virtual points can be converted to a public recognition, gift cards, discounts with customers, cash, vacation or bonus days. The results also include a better sense of camaraderie and more motivated teams. Try this tactic! It's very easy to implement. The results are immediate and long lasting.

Rewarding outstanding service should not be a difficult task.

YOU can create a culture of recognition, tailor rewards to individuals, provide growth opportunities, and encourage peer recognition. Once those programs are established, then you can regularly reward those who provide outstanding service.

Related Books

Gray, D. (2019). *Objectives + Key Results (OKR) Leadership; How to Apply Silicon Valley's Secret Sauce to Your Career, Team or Organization.* Gray Publications.

Pruitt, J.D. & Condit, R. (2014). *Level Headed; Inside the Walls of One of the Greatest Turnaround Stories of the 21st Century, 2nd Ed.* Wheat Mark.

Robbins, T. (2016). *MONEY Master the Game; 7 Simple Steps to Financial Freedom.* Simon & Schuster

Robbins, T. (2017). *Unshakeable; Your Financial Freedom Playbook Creating Peace of Mind in a World of Volatility.* Simon & Schuster.

Twist, L. (2017, 2nd ed). *The Soul of Money; Transforming Your Relationship With Money and Life.* Norton

8. Provide performance feedback for your direct reports and teams.

This is one of the MOST important behavior for **adult learners,** based on my learning system research to date.

Feedback leads to learning.

That fact may seem obvious, but most people struggle with performance feedback.

When you look in the mirror you get immediate feedback. Right?

When you use digital mirrors, like screens on Zoom or Microsoft Teams meetings, you get behavior-based feedback from others. If someone rolls their eyes or expresses frustration in the chat, then you can respond immediately.

What about when YOU need to provide performance feedback to your direct reports?

Too many people struggle with performance feedback. **Many have never been taught HOW to provide professional feedback.**

And in a family system, where emotional memories linger for decades, many people avoid conflict. Or they create conflict. Or they practice bad communication or cause reputational damage.

My goal is for YOU to learn from those mistakes, so that you can be a better manager or leader.

Leaders, by definition, influence the behavior of followers toward a better vision. The core skill of leaders is public optimism. When YOU are in front of the room, or leading a discussion, then you are wearing your Leader Hat.

Managers, by definition, maximize the productivity of others. The core skill of managers is coaching, which requires performance feedback for your direct reports. When YOU are meeting in a 1:1 coaching session, then you are wearing your Manager Hat.

Here are some comments from frustrated Family Business leaders. Use these comments as "red flags" or "yellow flags." If you hear them, then use these comments as a trigger to have a conversation with someone. Today.

"I often feel like I'm in the dark. I wish I could get some feedback from my manager. I keep looking for new jobs on Linked In and job boards."

"My manager said "good job" in passing the other day. I have no idea what she was referring to."

"My friend works at a bigger company where they have affinity groups for women, Hispanics, military veterans, and she says those discussions help her find a place in the organization. I don't know how to keep motivated."

YOU can develop the skill of performance feedback by using these practical tips. Today! Give them a try!

1. **Be Timely and Specific**

    When you leave a restaurant after a great meal, that is the best time to compliment the waiter and the chef.

    When one of your direct reports does good work or bad work, the best time to provide feedback is immediately!

    A good guideline is to celebrate and compliment others in public. Always.

    When YOU need to discuss negative behavior or emotional topics, **always meet in private.** But do not wait! Schedule a 1:1 immediately.

    The rule is to **make sure that your comments are based on specific behaviors- what others say or do**.

    Conflict results when people make judgements or opinions that are not associated with actual behaviors. We make judgements in a milli-second and they are surprisingly accurate. Fill in the blanks here:

    The person who served you at that bar or restaurant last week was...
    When your sibling should have...
    When the owners could have...
    Or (one of my favorites), I still regret when I...

    One reason for making those judgements in a milli-second is to **protect our interests.** If someone threatens your parents or a loved one, then you will react in a milli-second to defend them. The oldest part of your brain gets triggered and you blurt some slander like "You're wrong!" or some defense, like "No way!"

Wouldn't life be easier if, instead, YOU always use the front of your brain to regulate what you say and do, so that you never say the wrong thing? See the comments above on "Trigger- Pause- Response" and "Ready- Fire- Aim" for some practical tips on how to "Practice the Pause."

In a similar way, **rumors from others** need to be addressed immediately, so that they are not repeated. Rumors are how people socialize ideas- based on a desired truth or a perceived truth. The rumor may or may not be true! Researchers know that the value of rumors is to socialize ideas. But there is NO value to rumors when providing performance feedback.

All of your direct reports deserve to know what they're doing well and what they need to work on. That's why YOU need to stay **focused on specific behaviors- what others say or do.**

2. Balance Positive and Constructive Feedback

Muscles contract and relax. Every exhale leads to an inhale. Day time leads to night time. Winter leads to Summer.

In every natural system, there is always a tension between opposing forces.

In the same way, people learn best when given both positive and negative feedback. That **positive feedback reinforces desired behaviors**, which is why you often start emails and meetings by expressing gratitude or "Thank you for…"

Negative feedback describes the behaviors that YOU do not want to reinforce, such as rudeness or disrespect.

Researchers also make a distinction between **constructive feedback,** which constructs a positive outcome, and **destructive feedback**, which leads to negative outcomes.

Constructive feedback builds to a better future or focuses on a positive, prosocial behavior. When you express kindness or compliment your sister for taking care of your grandmother, that is constructive feedback.

Destructive feedback is when you diminish someone by stating something negative. A common example is social media, where outrageous, destructive, negative comments are perpetuated. And the destructive effects of too much social media, including anxiety, depression, suicidal ideation, and social isolation, are well researched. The word "toxic" avoids definition, but "You know it when you see it." Destructive feedback destroys dreams.

You need to provide all three types of feedback: positive, negative and constructive feedback. And you need to avoid destructive feedback.

How much good feedback should you provide? Some researchers made silly claims that ratios work well; for instance, after five positive comments people may be more inclined to accept one bit of constructive feedback. But that ratio idea is not valid, and it creates artificial, forced feedback sessions. The best performance feedback is based on what others say and do. **Just the facts.** That's a simple rule. You can adopt that rule.

In some cultures, like the U.S., too much feedback is indirect and positive. You can avoid that **positivity bias** by providing direct feedback that is based on observed behaviors and performance.

What do you think of these examples?

"When you interrupted your brother from speaking, he was not able to finish his sentence."

"When you complimented George in front of his team I noticed that he smiled and thanked you."

The bottom line: **Balance is essential when providing performance feedback.**

3. Foster a Feedback Culture

Managers need to model a learning system by asking for feedback.

You can ask for feedback. You can also ask for advice.

I have taught this simple model for decades. Schedule a regular 30-minute 1:1 session and adopt the **10:10:10 structure.** In the first 10 minutes, the manager states their agenda items, because managers need to maximize the productivity of others. In the second 10 minutes, the direct report states their agenda items, and knows that their items are important. In the last 10 minutes, they both develop action steps to achieve their desired outcomes.

If the meeting time is only 3 minutes, the same process can be applied in a **1:1:1 structure.** Try it.

Feedback is the currency of all learning systems. A feedback culture can be defined as "what happens when the manager is not looking" and "how we share information and make decisions."

There is plenty of hype about the word **"culture."** Psychologists describe organizational culture in three ways. **Underlying assumptions** are the unstated beliefs, like "when Grandpa speaks, that's what we do."

Stated Values are the shared beliefs, like customer service or honesty, that describe your unique family business. **Artifacts** are the physical statements etched on your business card or website or the office lobby wall. Artifacts can also be behaviors or rituals or norms, like Summertime Friday hours or dress codes.

As you think about your organization, **here are some simple guidelines for you to develop your feedback culture**.

1. **Underlying assumptions-** everyone on our team is important
2. **Stated values-** we celebrate efficiency by reducing costs, daily 5-minute stand up meetings, weekly 1:1 sessions
3. **Artifacts-** when teams exceed goals, everyone gets rewarded

That's a simple guideline for creating a feedback culture. What you develop will be better, because your performance feedback culture will always improve.

One more point: your feedback cadence should mirror your business needs. Behavioral feedback should be immediate, because it focuses on what people say or do. Performance feedback can be weekly or quarterly, because it focuses on goals, missions, team activities. Annual feedback should mirror individual and team learning measures, such as career aspirations and career opportunities.

Great managers **model providing and receiving feedback**, so that everyone shares their expertise, listens to new ideas, and practices innovation. YOU can practice those skills!

4. Use a Growth Mindset Approach

Notice how you respond to this famous quotation from Peter Drucker:

"The purpose of business is to create and keep a customer. Business has only two functions- marketing and innovation."

Marketing is described as how you attract new customers to your product or service.

Innovation is described as a new idea, applied. Marketing uses narratives. Innovation uses experiments.

I love this quotation because it forces people to ask, is that accurate? What do I really think about the purpose of business?

The purpose of performance feedback is to reward desired behaviors and help people develop. Whatever you choose to say or do reflects your mindset.

A **fixed mindset** occurs when people say "I'm not willing" or "that won't work here" or "that's a simplified view of business..."

A **growth mindset** occurs when people say the opposite, such as "I'm willing to try something new" or "what would happen if we focused on marketing and innovation in our business?"

When providing performance feedback, **good managers often frame the session** with phrases such as "Next time I want..." or "Here are some resources for you..."

Feedback sessions always look in the rear view mirror, back in time.

Feed forward sessions look through the front windshield, forward in time. One of my favorite questions is "**What advice do you have for me?**" Advice is future-oriented, and always reflects a growth mindset. What would happen if you were to ask for advice from others?

"What advice do you have for me on this project?"

There is abundant research indicating that people flourish when they encouraged to grow in new ways. We are more like clay (capable of being shaped into something) than bricks (used for only a few purposes). And we are more like plants in a garden, reaching toward sunlight, than rocks in a garden.

When YOU **practice a growth mindset** you believe that your talents can be developed and you will achieve more than those with a fixed mindset.

Think of someone who coached or mentored you to be more successful. That person was competent and capable, and whatever **performance feedback they provided enabled you to flourish.** They helped you be even more confident and capable. So why wouldn't YOU imitate their good behavior?

Growth mindsets require curiosity and a willingness to experiment. Awareness and action. Knowing and showing.

Innovation leads to competitive advantages. You need to apply new ideas all the time. Your markets change regularly. Your supply chain resources change weekly. Your technology changes daily. They all require that YOU practice a growth mindset. Ask for some advice or performance feedback today!

Providing effective performance feedback is an essential skill.

Practice leads to improvement. Practice does NOT make you perfect, that's another silly myth. Adult learners need to try something, get feedback, then try something else. Learning is a haphazard process.

You can be timely and specific, balance positive and constructive feedback, foster a feedback culture, and use a growth mindset approach, immediately.

Feedback is the currency of learning. Performance feedback is a powerful tool for driving growth, enhancing team dynamics, and helping individuals flourish. Start today!

Related Books

Brickell, F.C. (2019). *The Cartiers; The Untold Story of the Family Behind the Jewelry Empire.* Ballantine.

Diamandis, P. & Kotler, S. (2020). *The Future is Faster Than You Think; How Converging Technologies Are Transforming Business, Industries, and Our Lives.* Simon & Schuster.

Dweck, C. S. (2006). *Mindset: The New Psychology of Success.* Ballantine Books.

Friedman, S. (2013). *Family Business and Positive Psychology; New Planning Strategies for the 21st Century.* American Bar Association.

Schuman, A. I(2011). *Nurturing the Talent to Nurture the Legacy; Career Development in the Family Business.* Palgrave Macmillan. New York. Part of the Family Business Leadership Series.

Chapter 5: The Ownership System

The Top Two Key Behaviors in the Ownership system:

9. Include active owners in financial distributions
10. Understand family shareholder dynamics.

"I've joined a cult that believes in high quality products, superior customer service and responsible corporate behavior. You should come to one of our meetings."

My Assumptions for the Ownership System:

1. Your core business(es) define your unique competitive advantage(s)
2. Your demand for responsible stewardship is endless and complex
3. Your talent development system needs accurate, practical data
4. Continual learning can accelerate your capacity for innovation, resilience and profitability

9. Include active owners in financial distributions

This is the MOST important behavior for **business owners**, based on my research to date.

Owners (active and passive) and non-owners need to know their roles so that distributions can occur without any confusion.

Too many Next Gen leaders **think they are active** owners, but they are passive owners or non-owners. That confusion can be reduced immediately. YOU need to understand these different roles so that you can reinforce them consistently.

Active owners have voting shares of an asset, and any related risks or rewards.

Passive owners do not have voting shares, but have an interest in an asset.

Non-owners, like non-family executive leaders, may have compensation tied to their performance that leads to a bonus or annual incentive.

Distributions are financial or equity assets that are transferred over time based on the ownership share percentage. When a business is profitable, the distributions may be paid. When the business is at risk or there is a significant threat, like COVID, then distributions may not be paid.

Most of my clients have written shareholder agreements so that everyone understands their role.

When I facilitate Next Gen meetings I often review their understanding using the **"What if…?" activity**. YOU can do this activity. Pick someone in the meeting. Then ask, "What if that person died this afternoon?" or "What if that person wanted to transfer their ownership to a non-family romantic partner?" Those "What if…?" questions often lead to lively discussions!

Here are some "yellow flag" comments from frustrated, lonely Family Business leaders. If YOU hear any of these comments, then please use them as triggers to state your thoughts and emotions.

"It's incredibly frustrating when our generation is "left out of the loop." I manage our personal investments and budgets. I manage our charitable giving. I don't understand why I'm not able to be part of the ownership meetings. The rumor is that they meet quarterly at our country club. But that's just a rumor."

"Not knowing the details makes me feel lonely. When the owners paid for grandma's assisted living situation I was relieved. But I would have taken care of her in our guest house, if only someone had asked me. I just don't understand why I was not included in that discussion."

Here are some tactics that YOU can implement immediately. Play with them!

1. Establish a clear dividend policy

   All family business leaders- whether family or non-family- need to trust that a fair policy serves the long term best interests of the owners, and rewards those who deserve to be rewarded.

   That **"perception of fairness"** is not always the same thing as fairness. If a cousin is not active in the family, or the business, and has a history of gambling, then you may ask, "Is it fair to give that cousin a distribution?"

   If someone is accustomed to receiving an annual distribution over $100,000 and the owners want to invest in the company, instead of providing that distribution, do active owners have a voice?

   All of my clients have different beliefs about transparency and fairness.

   There is a trend toward digital transparency, sometimes driven by millennials who want access to information. But active owners sometimes need to restrict access to information and keep it confidential.

   YOU need a written dividend policy that outlines how and when owners will receive financial distributions. Your policy needs to consider factors such as profitability, cash flow, and reinvestment needs.

   All owners should have a written copy.

   Non-family executive leaders should not expect to know those confidential policy details.

   One of my executive clients said, "I'm continually frustrated by the owners, who lack a clear vision for the business. For several years now, I've asked the owners and the board for a vision. They cannot provide one! So, our management team provides the terms for the owners and they tend to agree on how much we can compensate them. It may seem backwards, but it works for us."

My experience is that as businesses grow and the number of non-family executive leaders assume more responsibilities, then the need for written dividend policies will only get larger.

2. Communicate financial performance

Cash flow, asset protection, tax risks, estate laws, and market threats are not topics to ignore or "slip under the table" because "you don't need to know those stressful details." That would be irresponsible for any owner.

Next Gen leaders need to learn about financial performance so that YOU can make informed decisions.

One of the biggest factors in a successful continuity plan is **financial literacy.** And literacy can be developed at young ages. For instance, children who are old enough to earn an allowance may be expected to distribute those assets into three jars; one for charity, one for saving and one for spending.

In a similar manner, your active owners need to be informed about your financial performance on a regular basis. By definition, that is what all owners need to do!

Your financial management team (CEO, CFO, CPA, wealth advisors) must provide accurate financial statements, monthly reports, and updates that clearly explain the company's profitability and how it impacts financial distributions. One of my clients calls that "financial hygiene" because it's an endless, necessary process.

Internal and external audits are a common practice and a small expense. Spend the money for regular audits!

In ownership meetings another common practice is to include regular financial educational activities, perhaps led by a CFO, attorney, wealth advisor, or board member. The topics are endless, and may include growth, risk, profitability, liquidity, taxes, cybersecurity, philanthropy.

The point is to commit to ongoing financial literacy.

3. Involve active owners in financial decision-making

The purpose of a board is to advise and recommend.

The purpose of your financial team (CFO, accountants, wealth advisors, valuation advisor, attorney) is to advise and recommend.

The purpose of active owners is to take those recommendation and make decisions. Active owners not only need "a seat at the table." They need to understand risks, rewards, options, and multiple scenarios.

Passive owners may be encouraged to observe so that they develop financial literacy, and better understand HOW your owners make decisions.

I often review financial statements and ask about growth, risk, profitability, liquidity and charity in ownership meetings.

Case studies are the primary mode of instruction in college MBA programs for good reason- they force participants to develop skills by listening to different perspectives from others. The problem is that most case studies use available data from publicly traded companies- because that's all they can access. Increasing shareholder value may be a value of your family business. **But more likely, your family business owners want to perpetuate a legacy, reward loyal employees, or develop generational wealth.** Most wealth is generated by family businesses. And most philanthropy. And most innovation. Privately-owned businesses last longer on average than publicly-traded businesses. Those are some of the reasons why you require different case studies.

I frequently use case studies in family sessions, so that people can consider multiple perspectives, then make better informed decisions.

4. Educate active owners on financial matters

When one person makes a decision the results are often catastrophic.

When teams of active owners make decisions the results are usually well informed and profitable.

By definition, your active owners have a "vested interest" in the long term success of those decisions.

However, research in behavioral economics has identified biases in our decision making. We all have cognitive biases that affect us. When our favorite sports team wins, then we state "we won." And when our favorite sports team loses a game, then we distance ourselves from the outcome.

In the same way, we do whatever we can to avoid a perceived loss. For instance, if a patriarch wants to give $1M to a college or local museum, then the owners need to make sure that there is no significant risk to the business.

Today, there is more high quality, vetted information available online than at any time in history.

Next Gen leaders like you need to understand the financial aspects of the business by using formal tools, like workshops, seminars, classes or certificates.

And you need to use informal 1:1 sessions with your CFO or financial mentors to develop your financial literacy. Education on financial matters is endless.

Many of my clients develop financial literacy by creating a **Learning Journal**. Think of a spread sheet or Google folder. Start by listing key definitions or questions. Then do some research inside your organization. Determine WHO may be able to answer the question. If you can add an answer or digital reference, copy and paste that answer into your notes. Add a date, because the terms may change. If you need to do some research outside the organization, do the same thing. Then share your notes every two weeks with your manager or mentor on the financial leadership team.

At some larger organizations, new hires and recently promoted people are required to keep a Learning Journal. Then they have a reference book to share with others. Try it.

All active owners, by definition, need to be engaged in financial distributions. YOU may need to establish a clear dividend policy, communicate financial performance, involve them in decision-making, and provide financial education.

As technology accelerates, the speed of investing recommendations will only get faster.

Related Books

Dalio, R. (2017). *Principles*. Simon & Schuster.

Diamandis, P.H., & Kotler, S. (2012). *Abundance; The Future Is Better Than You Think (Exponential Technology Series)*. Free Press.

Diamandis, P. & Kotler, S. (2020). *The Future is Faster Than You Think; How Converging Technologies Are Transforming Business, Industries, and Our Lives*. Simon & Schuster.

Ismail, S., Diamandis, P.H., & Malone, M.S. (2023). *Exponential Organizations ExO 2.0; The New Playbook for 10x Growth & Impact*. Ethos Collective.

Robbins, T. (2016). *Money; Master the Game: 7 Simple Steps to Financial Freedom*. Simon & Schuster.

Robbins, T. & Mallouk, P. (2017). *Unshakeable; Your Financial Freedom Playbook Creating Peace of Mind in a World of Volatility*. Simon & Schuster.

Woodson, W.I. & Marshall, E.V. (2021). *The Family Office; A Comprehensive Guide for Advisers, Practitioners and Students*. Columbia Business School.

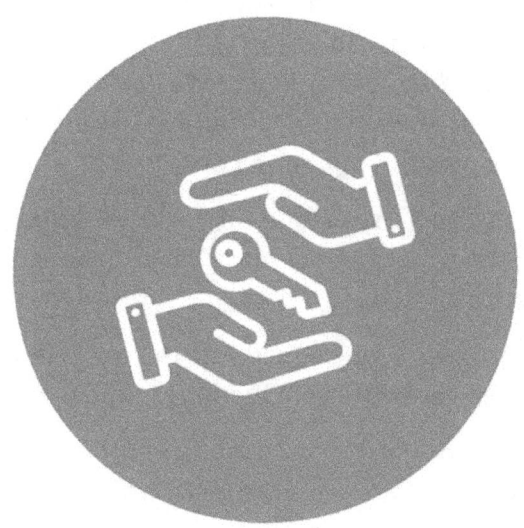

10. Understand family shareholder dynamics.

This is one of the MOST important behaviors for **business owners,** based on my research to date. Owners need to understand the complexity of governance.

Many family business owners have a verbal understanding of "what grandpa wants" or how to distribute shares. But **verbal understandings are NOT adequate.**

You need a shared understanding, and you probably need written guidelines for those decisions. **That process is called governance.**

Most families require a team of expert facilitators to help them make governance guidelines. YOU may already have some trusted experts including your accountant, attorney, wealth advisor, and a valuation consultant.

An **advisory board** may be good, as you scale up your business, because we all need teams of experts to provide advice.

A **fiduciary board**, with a majority of independent (non-family) members may be great as you increase complexity, because those directors will provide more objectivity and governance. Many of my clients require expert facilitators to identify key topics and minimize conflicts.

You probably have someone like Uncle Fred or Cousin Samantha who brings their own verbal understanding to your governance discussions.

What do you do when Uncle Fred says that his children deserve more shares, because they are working in the business?

What do you do when Cousin Samantha says that her children, who have struggled with alcoholism, deserve more shares because they need more support than others?

That's when you need to understand shareholder dynamics!

Here are some "yellow flag" comments from frustrated, lonely Family Business leaders. If you hear any of these comments, then please use them as triggers to state your thoughts and emotions.

"I hate family meetings. I often feel frustrated and overwhelmed by the drama games. The dynamics. I can't ever meet the expectations of my uncles, who are the majority owners. I wish I had an ally. I don't know how to navigate this terrain."

"I don't understand my in-laws. They provoke one another. The cousins pick fights with each other on petty issues or some special interest project. I feel like I'm alone on an island. And I certainly don't want to create even more drama or longer meetings."

Poker players distinguish between the "cards on the table," the shared observable facts, and the "cards under the table," the assumptions we make about others. You need to understand both levels of these dynamics before playing this game!

Here are some practical tips that YOU can implement today. Shuffle the card deck and let's play with them!

1. Educate yourself on family governance structures

In many Asian and European family businesses, the eldest son provides continuity. If the parents do not have a son, then they adopt one or arrange for their daughter to marry someone suitable. That structure, called **primogeniture, has perpetuated cultural values like harmony and continuity for thousands of generations.** And now it is dissolving in China.

In today's global, culturally diverse, digitally connected world, that pattern is changing because disempowered people now have new opportunities to express their thoughts and feelings.

In the U.S., more women are graduating from college then men, and those women have more expectations than ever. Just ask them!

When you ask your Next Gen leaders, both family and non-family, about governance, they probably want more transparency than the older generations want to share.

Thankfully, those governance structures are pretty easy to understand.

I typically start with an understanding of **shared values, a mission statement, a decision matrix, then a constitution or charter, and committees** designed to serve the family business over generations.

That process requires an expert consultant who knows the science (what works) and the art (what is needed). That consulting process is more complex than I can describe in this short Success Playbook. You will likely need an expert consultant to accelerate your governance and succession work. It's a small and necessary investment.

2. Foster open and transparent communication

Too often, when learning about a family in the discovery process, someone will ask, "Can you fix my brother?"

Truly. I can't make up this example because it's occurred too often!

(The answer is "No").

The fact is that communication is an endless process of idea exchanges (e.g., verbal, nonverbal, digital, real or imagined).

When you were a child you probably sat in the lap of some grandparent, who may have encouraged you to "play nice." But we do not actively teach people HOW to communicate better.

The result is that many of my clients perpetuate bad communication, simply because they don't know any better. Triangulation and gossip are as painful as avoidance. Social media and television perpetuate outrageous, bad communication.

The best model that I've taught for decades is called the **Complete Communication Wheel** (developed by a former business partner, Lloyd Raines. See the details in a previous chapter.)

You can start by asking, "May I have two minutes of your time?" Then you can state the data, one judgement, one emotion, the big want, and what we are willing to do. Then you can ask, "What would you like to do next?" After practicing that script in 1:1 coaching sessions, and taking notes, people are able to practice better open communication.

Then you can have regular meetings and discussions to address concerns, share information, and align on key decisions. To repeat, **effective communication is an endless process.**

Yes, YOU can get better at building trust and avoiding conflicts. Practice makes you better!

3. Define roles and responsibilities

Conflicts often occur when people disagree about goals or roles. If one owner wants to invest in the business, and another owner wants liquidity, then YOU will have different goals and likely have conflict.

That's why owners must have a decision-making process to agree on goals, what to focus on. **Those roles identify WHO does WHAT.** Every basketball game requires shooters and guards, but those roles may be filled by the shortest shooter or the slowest guard on the team.

In a similar way, roles define the responsibilities of shareholders within your business. Next Gen leaders under age 21 may adopt the role of observing board meetings or family councils.

Next Gen leaders over age 21 may adopt a passive owner role, until they exceed the family employment guidelines. Then they may apply for an open role within the business, or they may prefer a role outside the business.

Active owners may guide decision-making, manage conflicts, investments, finances, philanthropy, or performance reviews of executive leadership. Those roles need to evolve, and term limits often minimize potential conflicts.

Role descriptions, like any job description, are NOT engraved in granite!

The best model for team dynamics is hierarchical, called GRPI, and I've used it for decades.

The **G = Goals**, and it's critical that all participants understand and align with one goal, not more than one goal. The **R = Roles and Responsibilities.** As described above, roles change as people age and market conditions change. Roles need to be written and updated. The next **P = Process and Procedures.** These are the required or recommended steps to make decisions, or deliver your product or service or vision. If those three aspects are aligned, from G to R to P, then the **I = Interpersonal Interactions** should be a result. Too often clients say something like "Matt and Ted are in conflict." My experience is that when teams move from G to R to P, then the I works itself out.

One related point: we over-use the word "Teams." Teams have a shared goal and high level of commitment. Most work is NOT done by teams.

Most work is done in groups, defined as two or more people contributing some skill or resource. The marketing group creates some collateral. The sales group sells to new or returning customers. The accounting group sends the invoice and collects payment. The manufacturing group creates some product or service. The ownership group manages assets and risk. Most groups work at different times.

You may find it useful to focus on the Effectiveness or Efficiency or Outcomes (EEO) of each work group, rather than some vague notion of a team, because that's what each person can focus on.

The need to focus on family shareholder understanding is something that the active and passive owner groups should focus on. But they may never work as a team.

4. Seek external expertise

Show me any successful leader and I will ask, "Who is on their team?"

I often state, "**Teams win, and individuals fail.**

When trying to understand **shareholder dynamics**, there is too much complexity for any one person to "get the full picture."

Individuals are complex. **Groups of shareholders, each with a vested interest in real or potential asset distribution, are infinitely complex.**

Business psychologists, like me, lean on 100+ years of social science research to understand behaviors. But people are so complex!

Think of your last family meeting, whether it was at a kitchen table or a board table. Imagine that a video camera somehow recorded everyone at the table. Then imagine a team of experts tasked with describing the complexity they observed.

Person A may have spoken the most. Person B made the final decisions. And Person C slumped quietly in the corner.

Family dynamics can be studied, just like a scene from the movie "*Twelve Angry Men.*" Movie critics will focus on the cinema tactics. Linguists will focus on words and tone. Psychologists will focus on the behaviors.

In a similar manner, you may require an expert facilitator to study and mediate your shareholder dynamics. See the expert colleagues at www.theFBCG.com. Those professionals can provide objective insights, facilitate discussions, and offer guidance on best practices to navigate complex family dynamics.

Ask for help!

Your owners deserve such expertise!

The bottom line is that YOU need to understand family shareholder dynamics better. We all do.

You can educate yourself on family governance structures, foster open communication, define roles and responsibilities, and seek external expertise when needed.

Just like that poker game or basketball game, family dynamics are endlessly complex and require that you observe and act with care.

Related Books

Agrawal, A., Gans, J. & Goldfarb, A, (2018). *Prediction Machines; The Simple Economics of Artificial Intelligence.* Harvard Business Review Press.

Grant, A. (2021). *Think Again; The Power of Knowing What You Don't Know.* Viking.

Jaffe, D.T. (2020). *Borrowed From Your Grandchildren; The Evolution of 100-Year Family Enterprises.* Wiley.

Jennings, J.M. (2023). *The Uncertainty Solution; How to Invest with Confidence in the Face of the Unknown.* Greenleaf.

Kahneman, D. (2011). *Thinking fast and slow.* Farrar, Straus and Giroux.

Maurya, A, (2016). *Scaling Lean; Mastering the Key Metrics for Startup Growth.* Portfolio Books.

Next Steps

In the final pages of any book, there's a temptation to summarize key points into takeaways that YOU can use like a checklist.

Instead, here are the First Steps, repeated for your convenience, plus some notes. You can do this!

1. Take the self-rater or 360 Leadership Assessment survey at www.AssessNextGen.com to identify your strengths, weaknesses, blind spots/gaps, and hidden strengths. Or go to https://www.nextgenpeergroups.com/gifts

2. List your highest scores, your top 3-4 strengths here so that you stay focused on developing them:

_____

_____

_____

_____

3. List your lowest scores, your bottom 3-4 weaknesses here so that you can focus on developing them:

_____

_____

_____

_____

4. Use the Personalized Learning Plan (PLP) in the Appendix to
   - Practice with your consultant or accountability coach
   - Practice with your Next Gen Peer Group network (see details at www.NextGenPeerGroups.com)

- Practice with your colleagues
- Practice with your family/friends/champions
- Develop these behaviors ASAP
- Celebrate at each milestone!

5. The Next Gen model describes your skeletal system. Your family business or enterprise is uniquely complex. You are unique and complex. And you provide the life blood for your next steps.

Here are the two central questions for you:

1. **How do I fit in?** Use your low scores and high scores to assess where you are today. Practice improvement.

2. **What is my capability?** Select any of these 10 behaviors, then practice any of the recommendations. You have unlimited potential!

Appendix 1. Your Personalized Learning Plan (PLP)

My Personalized Learning Plan (PLP) - Confidential

My name: _____ Date: _____

Task: Take notes on ANY of the behaviors that YOU want to develop for ANY of these 5 systems. Add a date. Share it with your accountability partner, manager, coach. Include the action and any required resources. Then review your progress after 3 months.

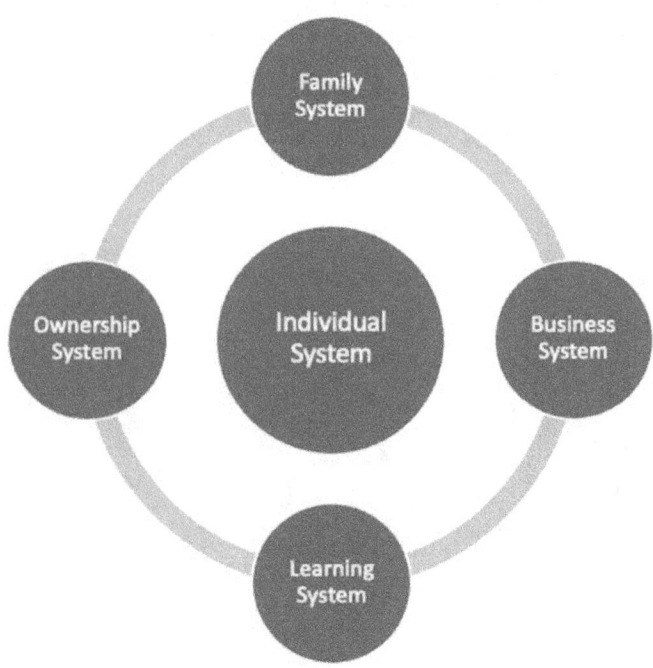

Appendix 2. Assumptions for the Five Systems

These 20 assumptions were critical when I developed the theoretical model, and the 50 sample items. I wanted to list these 20 assumptions in this appendix, because they reflect my beliefs, and shape all of the content described in this playbook.

Individual System:
1. You have agency/ choice
2. You have the capacity to flourish
3. Your individual awareness drives your behaviors and career(s)
4. Practicing leadership requires both knowing/awareness and showing/actions

Family System:
5. Your elders have shared values, assumptions, behaviors that may be stated/ unstated
6. Your current family will change over time
7. How you communicate, make decisions, and address conflict can be improved
8. You need a safe process for assessing and developing the unique strengths of your key leaders

Business System:
9. Your global, networked market demands will increase in complexity
10. Your technology-based solutions will define your success

11. Your working teams are the fundamental units in all successful businesses
12. Great managers maximize the productivity and profitability of others

Learning System:

13. Your curiosity is innate and can be nurtured
14. Practicing personal mastery is the cornerstone of your learning organization
15. Your mental models are like videos of your potential
16. Great leaders co-create a shared vision of a better future

Ownership System:

17. Your core business(es) define your unique competitive advantage(s)
18. Your demand for responsible stewardship is endless and complex
19. Your talent development system needs accurate, practical data
20. Continual learning can accelerate your capacity for innovation, resilience and profitability

APPENDIX 3: THE LEADERSHIP 360 ASSESSMENT PROCESS

I always want to know, "What really works?" I am attracted to process models that are practical and have descriptive utility. These seven practical steps may be used as a study guide or training tool for consultants, advisors, Family Officers, Board leaders, Family Council members, or academics.[1] For each of the following steps there are case study examples, key words, key questions, and recommended resources in another book, *The Assess Next Gen^{TM} Process Guidelines*. The 360 Leadership Assessment Consulting Process is described at www.AssessNextGen.com and below.

What is the Assess Next Gen™ Consulting Process?

In response to client requests and a perceived market opportunity, Doug Gray, Ph.D. and Kent Rhodes, Ed.D. developed and validated a digital 360 consulting process for Next Gen Family Business leaders in 2022. We started with a theoretical model that reflects the complexity of family enterprises and the need for individual fit. Those five systems are familiar: the business, family, ownership, individual and learning system (see Figure 1 in the beginning of this Playbook). Systems theory is not new. However, psychometric validation of those five systems required that we identified 250 behavior items, then statistically reduced that number to 10 items in each system, using a global sample population. The result is a new validated 50-item behavior-based digital 360 assessment process for next generation family business leaders.[2]

360 assessments are the most valid performance feedback process known to organizational development psychologists.

These assessments are now defined by best practices that define rigor, confidentiality and relevance.[3] In our family business arena, the raters may have multiple roles. For instance, Uncle Bob may also be an owner and manager. This assessment process includes seven rater groups, and a hierarchy that reflects the complexity in many family enterprises. Uncle Bob should provide feedback as an owner (first). Those seven rater groups include owners, board members, managers, peers, direct reports, family/ friends, and self-raters. The overall scores (high and low behaviors) and the gaps between other ratings and self-ratings, are useful for the next gen leader, and the owners, to make strategic decisions. The consulting process is both quantitative (using at least 13 raters) and qualitative (using verbatim comments and behavioral interviews).

We have validated two versions: one for non-family leaders and one for family leaders. And we have a self-rater version for any leader in a family business. This leadership assessment process provides invaluable direction for a consultant, deep behavioral insight for the owners, models performance feedback and organizational change, and clarifies required behaviors for any decision-makers included in this process.

Our experience is that any advisors serving family enterprises, can benefit from a 360 leadership assessment process.[4] We now have process guidelines for consistent delivery of behavioral feedback. There is no more need for sleepless nights, either for owners or for Next Gen leaders. If you have any questions about using this process please see www.AssessNextGen.com or contact the authors.

1. These seven steps are adapted from Nieto-Rodriguez, A. (2021) in *The Project Economy Has Arrived.* Harvard Business Review, Reprint R2106B; Boston. The author has ties to the Project Management Institute, and in 2021 published *The Harvard Business Review Project Management Handbook*.
2. Gray, D.W. & Rhodes, K.B. (2022) *How Does Your Family Measure Up? Using Assessments to Develop Effective Leaders.* **https://www.thefbcg.com/resource/how-does-your-family-measure-up-using-assessments-to-develop-effective-leaders/**
3. *The Handbook of Strategic 360 Feedback.* Eds. Church, A.A., Bracken, D.W., Fleenor, J.W., & Rose, D.S. (2019). Oxford University Press; New York.
4. Gray, D.W. (2021). *Distributed Ownership Tips for Family Businesses.* https://www.thefbcg.com/resource/distributed-ownership-tips-for-family-businesses/

APPENDIX 4: FAMILY BUSINESS CONSULTING GROUP (FBCG) RESOURCES FOR YOU SORTED BY THE FIVE SYSTEMS

Individual System

- https://www.thefbcg.com/resource/from-partners-by-chance-to-partners-by-choice-the-7-cs-of-trust-based-partnerships/
- https://www.thefbcg.com/resource/the-family-business-is-not-a-life-sentence/
- https://www.thefbcg.com/resource/family-champions-energy-for-success/
- https://www.thefbcg.com/resource/getting-unstuck/
- https://www.thefbcg.com/resource/please-welcome-to-the-stage-in-their-new-role/

Webinar:

https://www.thefbcg.com/resource/we-are-the-champions-developing-family-leaders-to-sustain-the-family-enterprise/

Webinar | Who am I: Helping Next Gen Find their Place in the Family Enterprise

Family System

- https://www.thefbcg.com/resource/durable-family-harmony-the-beacon-for-strong-family-businesses/
- https://www.thefbcg.com/resource/building-family-harmony-starts-with-living-our-values/
- https://www.thefbcg.com/resource/the-learning-family-how-to-manage-communication-toxins-in-family-relationships/

- https://www.thefbcg.com/resource/team-building-in-the-next-generation-preparing-future-leaders-2/
- https://www.thefbcg.com/resource/dear-family-business-advisor-answers-to-top-questions-about-family-meetings/
- https://www.thefbcg.com/resource/what-do-family-councils-do/
- https://www.thefbcg.com/resource/family-wealth-continuity/

Webinar:

https://www.thefbcg.com/resource/durable-family-harmony-smoother-sailing-to-family-business-success/

Book:

https://www.thefbcg.com/resource/family-champions-and-champion-families-developing-family-leaders-to-sustain-the-family-enterprise-2/

Business System

- https://www.thefbcg.com/resource/what-makes-for-a-great-family-business-board/
- https://www.thefbcg.com/resource/family-businesses-need-legal-documents-that-go-beyond-estate-plans/
- https://www.thefbcg.com/resource/should-we-hold-sell-or-consolidate-ownership-of-the-family-business-navigating-the-discussion-and-decision-process/
- https://www.thefbcg.com/resource/risk-management-a-multi-faceted-challenge/
- https://www.thefbcg.com/resource/understanding-profitability-in-the-family-business/

- https://www.thefbcg.com/resource/the-competitive-advantage-of-culture-in-a-family-business/

Learning System

Webinar: https://www.thefbcg.com/resource/we-are-the-champions-developing-family-leaders-to-sustain-the-family-enterprise/

- https://www.thefbcg.com/resource/walk-the-talk-building-next-gen-communication-skills/
- https://www.thefbcg.com/resource/the-learning-family-building-a-familys-capacity-to-develop-as-a-team/
- https://www.thefbcg.com/resource/the-family-that-learns-together-stays-together/
- https://www.thefbcg.com/resource/developing-a-family-enterprise-owners-mindset/
- https://www.thefbcg.com/resource/the-five-fundamental-building-blocks-of-strong-family-businesses/
- https://www.thefbcg.com/resource/rotational-systems-an-approach-to-career-development/
- https://www.thefbcg.com/resource/welcoming-up-and-comers-of-the-next-generation/

Webinar:

https://www.thefbcg.com/resource/are-we-all-in-agreement-effective-decision-making-in-family-businesses/

Book:

https://www.thefbcg.com/resource/family-education-for-business-owning-families-strengthening-bonds-by-learning-together/

Ownership System

- https://www.thefbcg.com/resource/optimizing-ownership-values-vision-goals/
- https://www.thefbcg.com/resource/the-five-fundamental-building-blocks-of-strong-family-businesses/
- https://www.thefbcg.com/resource/family-businesses-need-legal-documents-that-go-beyond-estate-plans/
- https://www.thefbcg.com/resource/family-owner-development-the-foundation-for-continuity/
- https://www.thefbcg.com/resource/getting-into-the-horizontal-box-aligning-family-business-owners-2/
- https://www.thefbcg.com/resource/solving-the-puzzle-of-ownership-alignment-in-a-family-enterprise/
- https://www.thefbcg.com/resource/owners-by-choice/

Webinar:

https://www.thefbcg.com/resource/three-key-conversations-for-sibling-partnerships-to-succeed-in-succession/

Books:

https://www.thefbcg.com/resource/family-business-ownership-how-to-be-an-effective-shareholder/

https://www.thefbcg.com/resource/family-business-succession-your-roadmap-to-continuity/

APPENDIX 5: MY PUBLISHED ARTICLES

Gray, D.W. & McVeigh, N. (November 15, 2023). *Family Business Leadership 360 Assessments: Case Studies on the Art of Experience and the Science of Data-Driven Decision Making.* Family Firm Institute, Practitioner. Retrieved from https://digital.ffi.org/editions/family-business-leadership-360-assessments-case-studies-on-the-art-of-experience-and-the-science-of-data-driven-decision-making/

Gray, D.W. & Rhodes, K.B. (2022) *How Does Your Family Measure Up? Using Assessments to Develop Effective Leaders.* https://www.thefbcg.com/resource/how-does-your-family-measure-up-using-assessments-to-develop-effective-leaders/

Gray, D. (2023, March 24). Assessments can help develop family business leaders. FamilyBusiness.org. Retrieved April 9, 2023, from https://familybusiness.org/content/assessments-can-help-develop-family-business-leaders

Assessments, tests, and evaluations are being used more routinely in businesses, and new tools are coming on the market designed specifically for family firms. In our consulting work with families and their enterprises, we've seen that assessments can help firms clarify individual and organizational needs and deeply inform the next steps that family leaders and company directors should take.

Assessments give family firms a source of objective data or information for higher quality decision making. They can be helpful as enterprise leaders consider a family member for promotion within the business, a next generation member's leadership capability and development needs, a family member's potential governance roles within various enterprise boards (business, family council, foundation, etc.), or as a way for families to identify and improve communication habits.

For example, one of our clients identified five mid-level candidates for their next generation of leadership. The company was growing 40% each year and the current president and CFO were ready to move on, so the client needed to assess the strengths of these five candidates and get ready for the transition. We developed a customized, confidential 360-leadership development assessment process that included both quantitative feedback (e.g., ranking on 50 scientifically validated behavioral items) and qualitative feedback (e.g., semi-structured interviews asking "what should this leader start, stop, and continue doing?") The assessment resulted in a 34-page detailed report summarizing the feedback from seven different rater groups (e.g., owners, board, managers, peers, direct reports, family/friends and self) and specific behaviors that could be implemented immediately. More than 50 people provided this performance feedback, which made them more ready for the transition and guided the company's decisions about promotions, re-assignments, and new hires. (For details see www.AssessNextGen.com.)

Business Assessments 101

Assessments take on various forms – from simple surveys or interviews to complex, statistically robust, multi-rater reporting. Our business, the Family Business Consulting Group, uses a simple form of assessment at the beginning of an engagement by conducting interviews with family members to define what they need and how we might be able to help. Answering the questions helps family members clarify their primary concerns and current challenges as well as the qualities they are looking for in a consultant. The FBCG team then utilizes this information to confirm stated needs and goals and to propose a way forward.

In fact, if family business consultants were asked to distill the steps of their work with families and their enterprises into one sentence, that answer would very likely include 1) assessing, 2) recommending, 3) supporting. Assessing the strengths and needs of both family and business(es) is the foundation of our recommendations for individual and family support and organizational change. The challenge has been that few tools expressly measure and assess the needs of families associated with multi-generational enterprises.

Collecting Data for Better Decision Making

While simply talking with stakeholders can always provide good insights, a wide array of more formal tools helps business leaders generate the hard data that informs sound decision-making. From financial goals to employee satisfaction, auto repair to cybersecurity, one can find assessment tools to measure just about anything. For example, assessments help business leaders discover predictors of job success – not only the skills needed to perform basic tasks, but also less obvious factors like learning agility and collaboration.

Other tools provide insight into individual and team performance success and the gaps that may be preventing that success. Assessments that generate accurate information about the "softer" elements of effective leadership and human interactions are important in helping family businesses transition leadership and ownership to the next generation in increasingly complex environments. In continuity planning, the older generation may ask, "When is the best time to transfer ownership and control to these well-intentioned but naïve kids?" At the same time, the younger generation is asking, "What can I possibly do to demonstrate that I am capable of running this family business?"

Intuition, gut feeling, or even bias often guide decisions like these. The data from assessments of the next generation's leadership capacities can confirm or dispel intuition, guide sound strategic decision making for the family enterprise, and reduce the risk of family disagreements about those decisions.

Kinds of Assessments

Many personality and behavior-oriented tools can help individuals and teams better understand their unique traits and blind spots. Behavioral or personality related self-assessments like Myers-Briggs, DISC, Enneagram, Hogan, Strengths Finder, etc. are all designed to provide information about how an individual might typically respond or think in any given circumstance. This data can then be utilized to help that person identify and shift less desirable behaviors while deepening their understanding how they can increase their effectiveness. Self-reports can help individuals focus on performance outcomes (e.g., increased productivity and focus) or behavior outcomes (e.g., improved relationships and effectiveness). In our family business consulting engagements, we also use team assessments (e.g., customized 360 leader assessments) to increase team strengths while managing potential conflicts.

Qualitative or Quantitative Assessments

Other types of measurement tools are useful as well. Qualitative assessments use words, pictures or digital content to describe a behavior or performance while quantitative assessments use numbers to describe a behavior or performance. Both are helpful in different ways. For example, when watching any sporting event there are often multiple commentators. One person provides the play-by-play and qualitative narrative. The second person provides the statistical comparisons and quantitative data.

Personal Assessments

Individual assessments, like those previously mentioned, focus on an individual's behavior or performance outcomes. For example, when Mark is late to work or exceeds a sales goal, an individual self-report of personality assesses what Mark thinks, even though that may be inaccurate or inflated. Team assessments focus on the commonly shared behavioral or performance outcome of a group. An example would be Mark's team engagement scores or team retention score after 12 months, or a milestone related to Mark's family business continuity planning.

Multi-Source Assessments

Multi-rater or multi-source assessments typically ask leaders to solicit feedback from their managers, peers and direct reports in the form of 360 feedback reviews. That data is then shared in confidence with the participant and a plan of action forward is created based on the feedback provided. For example, a 4th generation family member who is being considered for a management position within the family enterprise might engage in an anonymous 360 process to determine blind spots and perceptions that might be addressed to ensure her success in the new position.

Values-Based Assessments

Values based assessments help families identify signature strengths that everyone agrees describe how the family flourishes when at their best. For example, a family that determined their top signature strengths included "gratitude, fairness and spirituality" were able to hone specific behavior practices by family members that were consistent with these strengths.

By definition, effective family leadership goes beyond managing a successful enterprise. It also includes managing the productive behavior of stakeholders – both family and non-family; providing clarity about the strategic direction they are going; and upholding stated values of both the family and of the enterprise. Great leaders understand the impact they have on each of those stakeholders and how to accurately "read-the-room." Assessing and developing these "softer" interpersonal complexities of leadership within the family enterprise – alongside more traditional types of benchmarking assessments – can provide solid data-driven evidence for the development and continuity of effective family leaders.

Conclusion

Through our ongoing work with complex family enterprises, we've seen that many factors affect planning for succession, governance, and leadership roles, particularly when family members are being considered for those roles. We believe families could benefit by utilizing assessments that provide additional data that can help them make sounder decisions about future leadership and governance – and ensure the continued success of the family's business, foundation, family office, or family council.

APPENDIX 6: BOOK LIST

Agrawal, A., Gans, J. & Goldfarb, A, (2018). *Prediction Machines; The Simple Economics of Artificial Intelligence.* Harvard Business Review Press.

Aronoff, C., McClure, S. & Ward, J. (2011, 3rd ed.) *Family Business Compensation.* Palgrave MacMillan, New York. Part of the Family Business Consulting Group Series.

Baron, J. & Lachenauer, R. (2021). *Harvard Business Review Family Business Handbook; How to Build and Sustain a Successful, Enduring Enterprise.* Harvard Business School Press.

Baumoel, D. & Trippe, B. (2016). *Deconstructing Conflict; Understanding Family Business, Shared Wealth and Power.* Continuity Media.

Beman, K., Knight, J. (2006). *Financial Intelligence; A Manager's Guide to Knowing What the Numbers Really Mean.* Harvard Business School Press.

Brickell, F.C. (2019). *The Cartiers; The Untold Story of the Family Behind the Jewelry Empire.* Ballantine.

Brown, B. (2015). *Daring Greatly: How the Courage to Be Vulnerable Transforms the Way We Live, Love, Parent, and Lead.* Penguin Books.

Dalio, R. (2017). *Principles.* Simon & Schuster.

Diamandis, P.H., & Kotler, S. (2012). *Abundance; The Future Is Better Than You Think (Exponential Technology Series).* Free Press.

Diamandis, P. & Kotler, S. (2020). *The Future is Faster Than You Think; How Converging Technologies Are Transforming Business, Industries, and Our Lives.* Simon & Schuster.

Doerr, J. (2018). *Measure What Matters; How Google, Bono and the Gates Foundation Rock the World with OKRs.* Penguin.

Dugan, A.M., Krone, S.P., Lecouvrie, K., Pendergast, J.M., Kenyon-Rouvinez, D.H., & Schuman, A.M. (2008). *A Woman's Place; The Crucial Roles of Women in Family Business.* Part of the Family Business Consulting Series.

Dweck, C. S. (2006). *Mindset: The New Psychology of Success.* Ballantine Books.

Finance for Managers (2002). Harvard Business Essentials Series. Cambridge, MA.

Frederickson, B.L. (2009). *Positivity; Top-Notch Research Reveals the Upward Spiral That Will Change Your Life.* Three Rivers Press.

Friedman, S. (1998). *The Successful Family Business.* Upstart Publishing.

Friedman, S. (2013). *Family Business and Positive Psychology; New Planning Strategies for the 21st Century.* American Bar Association.

Gordon, J. (2008). *The Energy Bus: 10 Rules to Fuel Your Life, Work, and Team with Positive Energy.* Wiley.

Grant, A. (2021). *Think Again; The Power of Knowing What You Don't Know.* Viking.

Grant, A. (2023). *Hidden Potential; The Power of Achieving Greater Things.* Viking Press.

Gray, D.W. (2018). Dissertation: *Positive Psychology Coaching Protocols; Creating Competitive Advantage for Leader Development.* ProQuest: Ann Arbor, MI.

Gray, D. (2019). *Objectives + Key Results (OKR) Leadership; How to Apply Silicon Valley's Secret Sauce to Your Career, Team or Organization.* Gray Publications.

Grubman, J. (2013). *Strangers in Paradise; How Families Adapt to Wealth Across Generations.* Self-published.

Grubman, J., Jaffe, D.T. & Keffeler, K. (2023). *Wealth 3.0; The Future of Wealth Advising.* Self-published.

Harms, T. (2018). *The 12 Questions that Keep Family Business Directors Awake at Night.* Mercer Capital.

Housel, M. (2020). *The Psychology of Money; Timeless lessons on wealth, greed and happiness.* Harriman House; New York.

Ismail, S., Diamandis, P.H., & Malone, M.S. (2023). *Exponential Organizations ExO 2.0; The New Playbook for 10x Growth & Impact.* Ethos Collective.

Jaffe, D.T. (2020). *Borrowed From Your Grandchildren; The Evolution of 100-Year Family Enterprises.* Wiley.

Jennings, J.M. (2023). *The Uncertainty Solution; How to Invest with Confidence in the Face of the Unknown.* Greenleaf.

Kahneman, D. (2011). *Thinking fast and slow.* Farrar, Straus and Giroux.

Kenyon-Rouvinez, D. & Ward, J. (2005). *Family Business Key Issues.* Palgrave. Part of the Family Business Consulting Series.

Kurzweil, R. (2006). *The Singularity is Near: When Humans Transcend Biology.* Penguin.

Kurzweil, R. (2013). *How to Create a Mind; The Secret of Human Thought Revealed.* Penguin.

LaMorte, B. (2022). *The OKRs Field Book; A Step-by-Step Guide for Objectives and Key Results Coaches.* Wiley.

Lansky, D. (2016). *Family Wealth Continuity; Building a Foundation for the Future.* A Family Business Publication.

Lederach, J.P. (2003). *The Little Book of Conflict Transformation; Clear Articulation of the Guiding Principles By a Pioneer in the Field.* Good Books

Luthans, F., Youssef-Morgan, C.M. & Avolio, B.J. (2007). *Psychological Capital; Developing the human competitive edge.* Oxford University Press; Oxford.

Luthans, F., Youssef-Morgan, C.M. & Avolio, B.J. (2015). *Psychological Capital and Beyond.* Oxford University Press; Oxford.

Maurya, A, (2016). *Scaling Lean; Mastering the Key Metrics for Startup Growth.* Portfolio Books.

McNeill, M (2020). *The Prosperity Playbook; Planning for a Successful Family Business Succession.* Redwood.

Nacht, J. & Greenleaf, G. (2018). *Family Champions and Champion Families: Developing Family Leaders to Sustain the Family Enterprise.* Palgrave.

Pendergast, J., Ward, J. & Brun de Pontet, S. (2011). *Building a Successful family Business Board; A Guide for Leaders, Directors, and Families.* Palgrave Macmillan; the Family Business Consulting Group Series. New York.

Pruitt, J.D. & Condit, R. (2014). *Level Headed; Inside the Walls of One of the Greatest Turnaround Stories of the 21st Century, 2nd Ed.* Wheat Mark.

Rhodes, K. & Lansky, D. (2013). *Managing Conflict in the Family Business: Understanding Challenges at the Interchapter of Family and Business.* Palgrave Macmillan, New York. Part of the Family Business Consulting Group Series.

Robbins, T. (2016). *Money; Master the Game: 7 Simple Steps to Financial Freedom.* Simon & Schuster.

Robbins, T. & Mallouk, P. (2017). *Unshakeable; Your Financial Freedom Playbook Creating Peace of Mind in a World of Volatility.* Simon & Schuster.

Schmeider, J. (2014). *Innovation in the Family Business; Succeeding Through Generations.* Palgrave. Part of the Family Business Publication Series.

Schuman, A. I(2011). *Nurturing the Talent to Nurture the Legacy; Career Development in the Family Business.* Palgrave Macmillan. New York. Part of the Family Business Leadership Series.

Seligman, M.E.P. (2011). *Flourish; A Visionary New Understanding of Happiness and Well-Being.* Atria; New York.

Seligman, M.E.P. (2018). *The Hope Circuit; A Psychologist's Journey From Helplessness to Optimism.* Public Affairs Books.

Twist, L. (2017, 2nd ed). *The Soul of Money; Transforming Your Relationship With Money and Life.* Norton

Walsh, F. (2016). *Strengthening Family Resilience; 3rd Ed.* The Guilford Press.

Ward, J. (2004). *Perpetuating the Family Business; 50 Lessons Learned from Long-Lasting, Successful Families in Business.* Palgrave.

Wells, D. (2020). *When Anything Is Possible; Wealth and the Art of Strategic Living.* Self-published.

Woodson, W.I. & Marshall, E.V. (2021). *The Family Office; A Comprehensive Guide for Advisers, Practitioners and Students.* Columbia Business School.

List of Key Definitions

Active listening = a communication practice that requires sharing understanding until the speaker feels validated

Active owners = people with voting shares of an asset, including risks or rewards

Advisory board = a group of trusted advisors who provide advice to owners

Aspirational goal = a big, unattainable vision of a better future

Aspirational behavior = an exceptional, remarkable behavior from people who exceed expectations

Behavioral script = a communication model used to state feelings, undesired behavior, and desirable behavior

Business system = a description of how people fit into a unique family system and deliver a valuable product or service

Complete Communication Wheel = a script with five parts: data, emotion, judgment, want, will, plus opening and closing questions

Conflict = a response to different data or perspectives. One conflict model uses stages of incompatibility, personalization, intentions, behavior and outcomes. Another conflict model describes the interaction between task, relationship and process.

Conflict management = the process of responding to others with degrees of assertiveness or cooperation

Constructive feedback = positive statements that focus on desired, prosocial behaviors

Culture = a model used to describe organizations, based on underlying assumptions, stated values and artifacts

Data = facts that are quantitative (using numbers) or qualitative (using images or words)

Decision Matrix = an organizational structure used to determine who needs Input (I), Responsibility (R) or Decision (D) on key topics

Destructive feedback = negative statements that diminish others, and should be avoided

Distributions = financial or equity assets that are managed and transferred over time

Empathy = the capacity of understanding another person's perspective

Employees = workers with compensation tied to their performance

External audit = an assessment process led by expert financial, legal or talent consultants

Family system = a description of how related people support their shared values and beliefs

Feedback = what others say or do that shapes personal learning

Fiduciary board = a group of expert advisors with financial responsibility for an asset

Fixed mindset = a belief opposing new ideas or behavior

Flow Optimization = a behavioral model describing the balance between challenge and skill

Formal learning = the process of using content to demonstrate mastery of a skill

G2 = second generation family members, G3 = third generation, and so on...

Governance = a shared understanding for decision making, usually with written guidelines

Gratitude = the behavior of expressing appreciation for the good things in life

GRPI = a hierarchical model of team dynamics based on Goals, Roles, Process, and Interpersonal Interactions

GRPL = a financial decision-making model using Growth, Risk, Profitability and Liquidity

Growth mindset = a belief of openness to new ideas or behavior

Individual system = a description of how people integrate skills and talents into a unique family system or career

Informal learning = the process of using available resources to master a skill or competency

Innovation = a new idea applied using experiments

KPIs = a hierarchical organizational leadership system based on Key Performance Indicators

Leaders = people who influence the behavior of followers toward a positive vision. The core skill of effective leaders is public optimism.

Learning Journal = an individual or team reference document with key questions, definitions, and resources

Learning System = a description of how people adapt to new information and fit into a unique family

Locus of control = the belief that people have control over internal or external triggers

Loss aversion = a cognitive bias that influences people to avoid any real or perceived loss

Managers = people who maximize the productivity of others. The core skill of effective managers is coaching.

Marketing = behaviors designed to attract new or returning customers to a product or service

Negative feedback = negative statements that describe undesired behaviors

Operational goal = a necessary measure for delivering a product or service

OKRs = an organizational leadership system based on Objectives and Key Results

Operational behaviors = the required behaviors from people who deliver a product or service

Ownership system = a description of how owners assess and manage the long-term assets of a family or business

Passive owners = people who have an interest in an asset but do not have voting shares

Perception of fairness = the shared belief that a fair policy serves the long term best interests of the owners and rewards desired behaviors

POL = a decision-making model of social capital and non-financial assets including Philanthropy, Opportunity and Legacy

Positive feedback = positive statements that reinforce desired behaviors

Positive regard = the deepest human yearning based on safety, connections and dignity

Positivity spirals = behavior that encourages people to broaden their options and build solutions

Primogeniture = an ownership practice of providing harmony and continuity to the eldest son

Psychological Capital = a personal or team development model which measures Hope, Efficacy, Resilience and Optimism

RACI Matrix = a project responsibility chart to determine who is Responsible, Accountable, Consulted or Informed on key tasks

RASA = a communication model based on receiving, appreciating, summarizing and asking

Relationship conflict = a description of the interpersonal interactions with others, that often perpetuate negativity

Resilience = the ability of individuals or groups to get through difficult times or circumstances

Risk avoidance = the willingness to avoid one behavior

Risk tolerance = the willingness to do one behavior instead of losing another related behavior

Self-awareness = a narrative from assessments or feedback that are reliable and valid

Self-deception = an inaccurate narrative based on low self-awareness or inaccurate feedback from others

Shareholder dynamics = the infinitely complex interactions between shareholders, each with a vested interest in real or potential assets

Social Capital = a measure of the tangible and intangible relationships between people

Task conflict = a description of the content necessary to function with others

Thomas-Kilman model = a behavioral response model to conflict including avoidance, accommodation, competition, collaboration or consensus

Three Good Things = an activity of reflection and writing three good things

Triangulation = the communication practice of sharing information indirectly when it should be shared directly

Twalking = the behavior of talking and walking

Value-Based Coaching = a process designed to structure key relationships, results and personal behaviors

10:10:10 design = a performance management structure for managers and direct reports

About the Author

Doug Gray, Ph.D., PCC, has always focused on Next Gen leadership development. In his early career he focused on independent school teaching, non-profit administration, and Outward Bound wilderness instruction. He has worked with over 10,000 leaders in multiple business sectors, schools and colleges, and families. Since 1997, as CEO of Action Learning Associates, his consultancy guarantees results using the globally validated AD-FIT™ protocol in workshops, assessments, and executive coaching. Since 2018, with the Family Business Consulting Group, he focused on leadership development, succession and governance. In 2022, he co-founded the Assess Next Gen 360 Leadership Consulting Process for Family Business Leaders. In 2023, he created the Next Gen Peer Group process.

Doug loves speaking and training leaders who "need a little structure or a gentle nudge."

He and his family live near Nashville, TN, USA.

CONSULTING SERVICES

For Family Business Consulting go to https://www.Action-Learning.com/

For leadership consulting, book bulk ordering information, or to request permissions, go to www.Action-Learning.com at 3482 Stagecoach Drive, Franklin, TN, USA.

For the self-rater assessment go to https://www.nextgenpeergroups.com/gifts

For book series discounts go to https://www.nextgenpeergroups.com/books

For assessments, consulting, and products go to https://assessnextgen.com/

To connect go to https://www.linkedin.com/in/doug-gray-phd/ or https://substack.com/@legacyleadership

Thank you for practicing Leadership Development!

www.ingramcontent.com/pod-product-compliance
Lightning Source LLC
LaVergne TN
LVHW012023060526
838201LV00061B/4428